MORE PRAISE FOR *CREATIVE THINKERING*

"*Creative Thinkering* is a wonderfully entertaining 'operator's manual' for your creative brain. Turn to any page, and the idea machine in your head can't help but start manufacturing new ideas!"
— Bryan Mattimore, author of
The Idea Engine and president of the Growth Engine Company

"A real gem…Thought-provoking and interactive, *Creative Thinkering* bridges the perception gap and opens up creative vistas — even for those who don't believe they have the creative gene. Packed with information about the nature of creativity and absolutely loaded with germane and fun visuals, it's access to creativity served up on a silver platter."
— Gregg Fraley, author of *Jack's Notebook*

"*Creative Thinkering* offers a fresh look at creativity, from spontaneous to deliberate. Based upon his extensive study of and professional work in creativity and creative-thinking tools, Michael Michalko has once again written an excellent book to help people discover their creativity — including how to better understand it and how to expand and deepen it too."
— Robert Alan Black, PhD, CSP, author of
Broken Crayons: Break Your Crayons and Draw Outside the Lines

"As much as I totally immerse myself in reading more about creativity, I always learn something new, fascinating, and very valuable from Michael Michalko. His newest book's focus on powerful conceptual blending techniques and his mind-expanding illustrations and experiments for the reader make this book a new standard of discovery and thinking excellence for the aspiring creative genius in all of us."
— Ray Anthony, innovation consultant and author of
F-A-S-T Forward — and Step on It!

"A superb book! Read *Creative Thinkering* and begin to apply it immediately. Your professional and personal life will be opened to new and unimagined possibilities."

— Connie Harryman,
President of the American Creativity Association–Austin Global

PRAISE FOR MICHAEL MICHALKO'S BOOK *THINKERTOYS*

"Will change the way you think."

— *Wall Street Journal*

"Shows you how to expand your imagination."

— *Newsweek*

"A special find. Period."

— *Executive Edge*

"A must-have book in any business setting."

— *Women in Business*

"Believe it or not, this wonderful book will have you challenging the impossible."

— *Nonprofit News*

"This book is a creative-thinking workshop in a book that will have your imagination soaring."

— *Chicago Tribune*

"This book shows you how to do what you think can't be done."

— *The Futurist*

CREATIVE THINKERING

ALSO BY MICHAEL MICHALKO

Cracking Creativity: The Secrets of Creative Genius
Thinkertoys: A Handbook of Creative-Thinking Techniques
Thinkpak: A Brainstorming Card Deck

CREATIVE THINKERING

Putting Your Imagination to Work

MICHAEL MICHALKO

New World Library
Novato, California

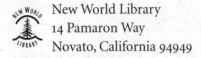 New World Library
14 Pamaron Way
Novato, California 94949

Text design by Tona Pearce Myers

Library of Congress Cataloging-in-Publication Data
Michalko, Michael, date.
  Creative thinkering : putting your imagination to work / Michael Michalko.
    p.   cm.
Includes bibliographical references and index.
ISBN 978-1-60868-024-5 (pbk. : alk. paper)
1. Creative thinking. 2. Creative ability. 3. Imagination. I. Title.
BF408.M485 2011
153.3'5—dc23   2011024369

4731 2276 10/11

First printing, September 2011
ISBN 978-1-60868-024-5
Printed in Canada on 100% postconsumer-waste recycled paper

g New World Library is a proud member of the Green Press Initiative.

10 9 8 7 6 5 4 3 2 1

To my wife, Anne, whom I married not because she is someone I could live with, but because she is the one person I cannot live without.

CONTENTS

PART 2. THE CREATIVE THINKER   143

ACKNOWLEDGMENTS

In Hanau, Germany, I met Franz, a Dutchman who had read my book *Thinkertoys*. He told me he worked for years as a middle manager for a major corporation. He was well paid and had an impressive title. Basically, he saw his job as little more than making workers into loyal company-team players. Each day, he felt his job becoming more and more meaningless, but he had difficulty imagining how he might earn a living otherwise.

My book *Thinkertoys* inspired him to learn as much as he could about creative thinking, and so he took a course on creative thinking at the University of Copenhagen. He began having all kinds of new ideas and creating innovative ways to do things in furniture design, even new ways to design stools and tables. Making furniture was his passion. And it was his awareness of his ability to think creatively that made him realize for the first time that he could change his life.

His professor at the university became excited about Franz's ideas for designing innovative, environmentally friendly furniture. The professor pushed him and pushed him until Franz quit his job and opened his own furniture design business, which has been hugely successful. Franz gave me a poem by Guillaume Apollinaire that he said reminds him of the professor who pushed him to live his dream.

"Come to the edge."
"We can't. We're afraid."
"Come to the edge."
"We can't. We will fall!"
"Come to the edge."
And they came.
And he pushed them.
And they flew.

I wish to acknowledge Franz's professor and all the people who teach others to become more creative in their business and personal lives. Among the best creative-thinking experts, teachers, trainers, and consultants in the world are Kelvin Fung (Hong Kong), Charles Prather, Terry Stickels, Peter Lloyd, Roger von Oech, Andre de Zanger, Bryan Mattimore, Edward de Bono, Joyce Wykoff, James Adams, Ray Anthony, Winston J. Brill, PhD, Robert Alan Black, PhD, Michael Gelb, Win Wenger, and Tony Buzan. These are among my heroes who teach people how to overcome their fears and doubts about their abilities, show them how to become creative thinkers, and push them over the edge to soar.

INTRODUCTION

Why are some people creative and others not?

The key question isn't "Why are some people creative and others not?" It is why in God's name isn't everyone creative? Where and how was our potential lost? How was it crippled? Why does education inhibit creativity? Why can't educators foster more creativity instead of less? Why is it that the more expert people become in their fields, the less creative and innovative they become? Why is it that people who know more create less, and people who know less create more? Why are people amazed when someone creates something new, as if it were a miracle?

We've been educated to process information based on what has happened in the past, what past thinkers thought, and what exists now. Once we think we know how to get the answer, based on what we have been taught, we stop thinking. The Spanish word for an "answer" is *respuesta*, and it has the same etymological root as *responso* (responsory), the song people sing to the dead. It's about what has no life anymore. In other words, when you think you know the answers, based on what has happened in the past, your thinking dies.

This is why, when most people use their imaginations to develop new ideas, those ideas are heavily structured in predictable ways by the properties of existing categories and concepts. Creative thinking requires the ability to generate a host of associations and connections between two or more dissimilar subjects, creating new categories and concepts. We have not been taught to process information this way.

CONCEPTUAL BLENDING

The key to creatively generating associations and connections between dissimilar subjects is conceptual blending. This is a creative-thinking process that involves blending two or more concepts in the same mental space to form new ideas.

Imagine, for a moment, that thought is water. When you are born, your mind is like a glass of water. Your thinking is inclusive, clear, and fluid. All thoughts intermingle and combine with each other and make all kinds of connections and associations. This is why children are spontaneously creative.

In school you are taught to define, label, and segregate what you learn into separate categories. The various categories are kept separate and not allowed to touch each other, much like ice cubes in a tray. Once something is learned and categorized, your thoughts about it become frozen. For example, once you learn what a can opener is, whenever someone mentions "can opener" you know exactly what it is.

You are taught, when confronted with a problem, to examine the ice cube tray and select the appropriate cube. Then you take the cube and put it in a glass, where your thinking heats and melts it. For example, if the problem is to "improve the can opener," the glass will contain all you have learned about can openers, and nothing more. You are thinking exclusively, which is to say you are thinking only about what you have learned about the can opener. No matter how many times the water is stirred, you end up creating, at best, a marginal improvement.

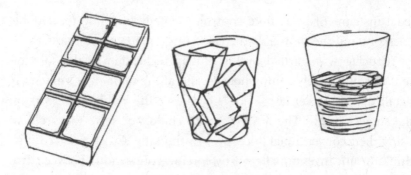

Now if you take another cube (for example, vegetables) and put it in the same glass with the can-opener cube, your thinking will heat and melt both together into one fluid. Now when you stir the water, more associations and connections are made and the creative possibilities become immensely greater. The vegetable cube, once blended with the can-opener cube, might inspire you to think of how vegetables open in nature. For example, when pea pods ripen, a seam weakens and opens, freeing the peas. This might inspire you to come up with novel ideas. You could, for example, manufacture cans with a weak seam that can be pulled to open the can. You cannot get this kind of novel idea using your conventional way of thinking.

What happens when you think simultaneously, in the same mental space, about a showerhead and a telescope orbiting the earth? When the Hubble telescope was first launched into space, scientists were unable to focus it. It could be salvaged only by refocusing it using small, coin-shaped mirrors. The problem was how to deliver the mirrors and insert them precisely into the right location. The right location was in a light bundle behind the main mirror. The NASA experts who worked on the problem were not able to solve it, and the multi-million-dollar Hubble seemed doomed.

Electrical engineer James Crocker was attending a seminar in Germany when he found out about the problem. He worked on it all day. Tired, he stepped into the shower in his hotel room. The European-style shower included a showerhead on an arrangement of adjustable rods. While manipulating the showerhead, Crocker suddenly realized that similar articulated arms bearing coin-shaped mirrors could be extended into the light bundle from within a replacement axial instrument by remote control. Mentally blending the Hubble telescope and the showerhead created this remarkable solution.

Crocker was startled by his sudden realization of the solution that was immensely comprehensive and at the same time immensely detailed. As Crocker later said, "I could see the Hubble's mirrors on the shower head." The NASA experts could not solve the problem using their conventional linear way of thinking. Crocker solved it by thinking unconventionally — by forcing connections between two remotely different subjects.

Look at the following illustration of the square and circle. Both are separate entities.

Now look at the extraordinary effect they have when blended together. We now have something mysterious, and it seems to move. You can get this effect only by blending the two dissimilar objects in the same space. The power of the effect is not contained in the circle or in the square, but in the combination of the two.

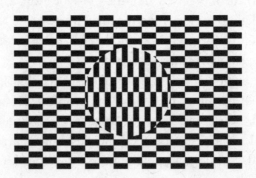

Creativity in all domains, including science, technology, medicine, the arts, and day-to-day living, emerges from the basic mental operation of conceptually blending dissimilar subjects. When analyzed, creative ideas are always new combinations of old ideas. A poet does not generally make up new words but instead puts together old words in a new way. The French poet Paul Valéry is quoted by mathematician Jacques Hadamard in *Jacques Hadamard, A Universal Mathematician*, by T. O. Shaposhnikova, as saying, "It takes two to invent anything. The one makes up combinations; the other one chooses, recognizes what he wishes and what is important to him in the mass of the things which the former has imparted to him." Valéry related that when he wrote poetry he used two thinking strategies to invent something new. With one strategy, he would make up combinations; and with the other, he would choose what was important.

Consider Einstein's theory of relativity. He did not invent the concepts of energy, mass, or speed of light. Rather, he combined these ideas in a new and useful way.

Think for a moment about a pinecone. What relationship does a pinecone have to the processes of reading and writing? In France in 1818, a nine-year-old boy accidentally blinded himself with a hole puncher while helping his father make horse harnesses. A few years later the boy was sitting in the yard thinking about his inability to read and write when a friend handed him a pinecone. He ran his fingers over the cone and noted the tiny differences between the scales. He conceptually blended the feel of different pinecone scales with reading and writing, and realized he could create an alphabet of raised dots on paper so the blind could feel and read what was written with it. In this way Louis Braille opened up a whole new world for the blind.

Braille made a creative connection between a pinecone and reading. When you make a connection between two unrelated subjects, your imagination will leap to fill the gaps and form a whole in order to make sense of it. Suppose you are watching a mime impersonating a man taking his dog out for a walk. The mime's arm is outstretched as though holding the dog's leash. As the mime's arm is jerked back and forth, you "see" the dog straining at the leash to sniff this or that. The dog and the leash become the most real part of the scene, even though there is no dog or leash. In the same way, when you make connections between your subject and something that is totally unrelated, your imagination fills in the gaps to create new ideas. It is this willingness to use your imagination to fill in the gaps that produces the unpredictable idea. This is why Einstein claimed that imagination is more important than knowledge.

Just as conceptual blending allows information to intermingle in the mind of the individual, when people swap thoughts with others from different fields this creates new, exciting thinking patterns for both. As Brian Arthur argues in his book *The Nature of Technology*, nearly all technologies result from combinations of other technologies, and new ideas often come from people from different fields combining their thoughts and things. One example is the camera pill, invented after a conversation between a gastroenterologist and a guided-missile designer.

THE BOOK

My purpose in writing this book is to emphasize the importance of conceptual blending in creative thinking in your business and personal lives. Conceptual blending of dissimilar subjects and ideas and concepts is the most important factor in creative thinking. The topics I discuss include the following:

- We are all born spontaneous and creative thinkers.
- How the thinking patterns inculcated in us by educators prevent us from using our natural creativity.
- Why geniuses are geniuses, and how geniuses use conceptual blending to create their novel ideas.

- How conceptual blending has inspired creative thinking throughout history, going back to the invention of fire.
- How to think differently by looking for analogical connections between the essences, functions, and patterns of dissimilar subjects.
- How to combine problems with random stimuli to create original ideas.
- How to change the way things are by changing the way you look at them.
- How to combine opposites and think paradoxically.
- How to combine "crazy" and "absurd" ideas with yours to provoke exciting new thinking patterns.
- The importance of incubating your thinking, and when to do it.

In the final three chapters, I hope to convey the three notable traits that all creative geniuses have in common:

- The importance of intention and how to use it to develop a creative mind-set.
- How to change your thinking patterns by changing the way you speak.
- How you become what you pretend to be.

The book's conclusion contains stories about human potential and people who have had the courage and will to overcome personal adversity. Interlarded throughout the book are thought experiments I've devised — a variety of questions to ponder, creative-thinking techniques, illusions, and puzzles to inspire your thinking.

I titled this book *Creative Thinkering*. The word *thinkering* is itself a combination of the words *thinker* and *thinking*. Enfolding the two words into the one word *thinkering* symbolizes how both the creative personality and the creative-thinking process, like form and content in nature, are inextricably connected.

THE BUTTERFLY EFFECT

You choose how to live your life. You create your own reality. You can choose to be an object in your life and let others tell you who you are and what you are capable of being. Or you can choose to be the subject in your life and determine your own destiny by transforming yourself into a creative thinker. This book will help you transform yourself, much as a caterpillar becomes a butterfly.

One day when I was ten years old, I was hiking up a hill to pick blackberries with Dido, my grandfather, when he stopped and picked up a caterpillar. "Look at this. What do you see?" "A caterpillar," I said.

"Someday this will become a beautiful butterfly. Look at it carefully and tell me what you see that proves this will be so." I studied the caterpillar carefully looking for a sign. Finally, I said, "Dido, there is nothing in the caterpillar that tells me it's going to be a butterfly." "Exactly!" my grandfather said. "And there is nothing in you on the outside that shows others what you will become. Remember this. When people tell you why you can't do something or become something, remember the caterpillar. You cannot see what is going on inside the caterpillar, and they cannot see what is in your heart or mind. Only you, like the caterpillar, know what you are capable of becoming."

I think of the caterpillar and butterfly when I think of how people can change. In metamorphosis, little things that biologists call imaginal cells begin to crop up in the body of the caterpillar. At first, they have difficulty surviving. It isn't until they begin to combine and interact with each other that they get stronger and are able to resist being attacked by the immune system. Then these imaginal cells replace the caterpillar cells, and the caterpillar becomes a butterfly.

I think that is a beautiful metaphor for the process of becoming a creative personality. We do not inherit our behavioral traits directly, through our genes. Instead we develop traits through the dynamic process of interacting with our environment. Think of these traits as your imaginal cells, which need to strengthen and change in order for you to become a creative person.

At first your changes may have difficulty surviving (much like the first butterfly cells), but over time — as you consistently work to change your perceptions, thinking patterns, speaking patterns, attitude, and the way you act — you will find these forces linking up and changing the way you interact with your environment. Like a caterpillar surprised when it becomes a butterfly, you will be surprised when you find yourself transformed from a dull, passive onlooker into an active creative thinker who can change the world.

PART 1
Creative Thinking

*I begin to wonder how many things I know would suddenly take on
new meanings if only I could perceive the connections.*

— ROBERT SCOTT-BERNSTEIN

We are educated to be analytical, logical thinkers. Consequently,
we have the ability to make common associations between
subjects that are related or at least remotely related. We are far better
at associating two things (for example, apples and bananas are both
fruits) than we are at forcing ourselves to see connections between
things that seem to have no association (for example, a can opener
and a pea pod).

Jeff Hawkins, in his book *On Intelligence*, explains how our ability
to associate related concepts limits our ability to be creative. We form
mental walls between associations of related concepts and concepts
that are not related. For example, if asked to improve the can opener,
we will make connections between all our common experiences and
associations with can openers. Our fixation with our common associations will produce ideas for can openers that are very similar to the
can openers that exist.

Developing the skill of forcing connections between unrelated things will tear down the walls between related and unrelated concepts. What connections, for example, can you force yourself to see between a can opener and a pea pod?

The function of a can opener is "opening." How do things in other domains open? For example, in nature a pea pod opens when a seam weakens as the pod ripens. Thinking simultaneously about a pea pod and a can opener in the same mental space will force a mental connection between the pea pod seam and a can opener. This inspires the idea of opening a can by pulling a weak seam (like the one in a pea pod). Instead of an idea to improve the can opener, we've produced an idea for a new can design. This idea is one you would never get using conventional thinking.

This is an example of conceptual blending, which is the act of combining, or relating, unrelated items in order to solve problems, create new ideas, and even rework old ideas. It succeeds because it is not possible to think of two subjects, no matter how remote, without making connections between the two. It is no coincidence that the most creative and innovative people throughout history have been experts at forcing new mental connections via the conceptual blending of unrelated subjects.

Part 1 of this book explores the nature of conceptual blending and gives practical examples of how to use this technique in a variety of different ways to inspire new ideas and solutions to problems.

ONCE WE WERE CREATIVE

Every child is an artist.
The problem is how to remain an artist
once we grow up.

— PABLO PICASSO

We were all born spontaneous and creative. Every one of us. As children we accepted all things equally. We embraced all kinds of outlandish possibilities for all kinds of things. When we were children, we knew a box was much more than a container. A box could be a fort, a car, a tank, a cave, a house, something to draw on, and even a space helmet. Our imaginations were not structured according to some existing concept or category. We did not strive to eliminate possibilities; we strove to expand them. We were all amazingly creative and always filled with the joy of exploring different ways of thinking.

And then something happened to us: we went to school. We were not taught how to think; we were taught to reproduce what past thinkers thought. When confronted with a problem, we were taught to analytically select the most promising approach based on history, excluding all other approaches, and then to work logically in a carefully defined direction toward a solution. Instead of being taught to look for possibilities, we were taught to look for ways to exclude them. It's as if we entered school as a question mark and graduated as a period.

Consider a child building something with a Lego construction set. She can build all kinds of structures, but there are clear, inherent constraints on the design of objects that can be made with the set. They cannot be put together any which way: they will not stay together if unbalanced and gravity pulls them apart. The child quickly learns the ways that Legos go together and the ways they don't go together. She ends up building a wide variety of structures that satisfy the toy's design constraints.

If the only constraint were to "make something out of plastic," and the child had at her disposal every method of melting and molding plastic, the currently possible Lego constructions would be only a tiny fraction of the possible products and would make the Lego constructions look contrived, not the result of motivation, when compared to her other products.

With Legos it is the constraints inherent in the design that limit what can be built. With us, it is the thinking patterns that formal education has firmly wired in our brains that limit our imagination and inventiveness.

Our mental patterns enable us to simplify the assimilation of complex data. These patterns let us rapidly and accurately perform routine tasks such as driving an automobile or doing our jobs. Habitual pattern recognition provides us with instant interpretations and permits us to react quickly to our environment. When someone asks you, "What is six times six?" the sum "thirty-six" automatically appears in your mind. If a man is born in 1952 and dies in 1972, we know immediately that the man was twenty.

Though pattern recognition simplifies the complexities of life, it also makes it hard for us to come up with new ideas and creative solutions to problems, especially when confronted with unusual data. This is why we so often fail when confronted with a new problem that is similar to past experiences only superficially, and that is different from previously encountered problems in its deep structure. Interpreting such a problem through the prism of past experience will, by definition, lead the thinker astray. For example, the man in the above example died at age forty-nine, not twenty. In this case, 1952 is the number of the hospital room where he was born, and 1972 is that of the room where he died.

In the following thought experiment, which taxi is out of order? See if you can solve it before you continue reading.

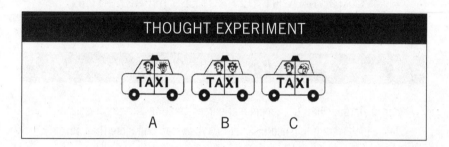

One of the hallmarks of a creative thinker is the ability to tolerate ambiguity, dissonance, inconsistency, and things out of place. Creative thinkers will look at problems many different ways and will examine all the variables involved, searching for the unexpected. For example, in the taxi problem, the letters *A*, *B*, and *C* are also considered part of the whole and not as separate labels. To solve the problem, move taxi C to the front of the line of letters to spell *cab*.

Our minds are marvelous pattern-recognition machines. We look at the illustration below, and our brains immediately recognize a pattern: we see the word *optical*. When we see something, we immediately decide what it is and move on without much thought.

Success at discerning patterns of one sort naturally lessens one's propensity to recognize patterns of another. Notice that once we recognize the word *optical*, we fail to recognize the word *illusion*. The more accustomed we are to reading a word as a stand-alone word with one meaning, the more difficult it is for us to recognize anything new or different about it. Namely, it is either optical or *not* optical. We do not pay attention to the background shapes. This is a standard aspect of reading. As a result, experts in "the standard of anything" may be those least qualified when it comes to developing or creating anything new.

WE ARE TAUGHT TO PROCESS INFORMATION
THE SAME WAY OVER AND OVER

THOUGHT EXPERIMENT

Martin Gardner had a phenomenal career creating several classic puzzles, which were published in *Scientific American* and more than seventy books. Following is one of them, a puzzle made with toothpicks.

Can you change "100" to "CAT" by moving just two of these toothpicks?

(Answer at end of chapter.)

This is difficult for many of us, because we are taught to process information the same way over and over again instead of searching for alternative ways. Once we think we know what works or can be done, it becomes hard for us to consider alternative ideas. We're taught to exclude ideas and thoughts that are different from those we have learned.

When confronted with a truly original idea, we experience a kind of conceptual inertia comparable to the physical law of inertia, which states that objects resist change; an object at rest remains so, and an object in motion continues in the same direction unless stopped by some force. Just as physical objects resist change, ideas at rest resist change; and ideas in motion continue in the same direction until stopped. Consequently, when people develop new ideas, these new ideas tend to resemble old ones; new ideas do not move much beyond what exists.

When Univac invented the computer, the company refused to talk to businesspeople who inquired about it, because, they said, the computer was invented for scientists and had absolutely no business applications. Then along came IBM, who captured the market. Next the experts at IBM, including its CEO, said that they believed, based on their expertise in the computer market, there was virtually no market for the personal computer. In fact, their market research indicated that no more than five or six people in the entire world had need of a personal computer.

Interestingly, one of the rules taught to students seeking a master's degree in business administration is that surprise should be minimized in the workplace. Much of what is taught to MBA candidates is aimed at reducing ambiguity and dissonance to promote predictability and order in the corporation. Yet if these rules had always applied to businesses, we would not have disposable razors, fast-food restaurants, copier machines, personal computers, affordable automobiles, FedEx, microwaves, Wal-Mart, or even an Internet.

Even when we actively seek information to test our ideas to see if we are right, we usually ignore paths that might lead us to discover alternatives. This is because educators discouraged us from looking for alternatives to the prevailing wisdom. Following is an interesting experiment, originally conducted by the British psychologist Peter Wason, that demonstrates our tendency not to seek alternatives. Wason would present subjects with the following triad of three numbers in sequence.

2   4   6

He would then ask subjects to write other examples of triads that follow the number rule and explain the number rule for the sequence. The subjects could ask as many questions as they wished without penalty.

He found that almost invariably people would initially offer the numbers "4, 6, 8" or "20, 22, 24" or some similar sequence. And Wason would say, yes, that is an example of the number rule. Then they would offer something like "32, 34, 36" or "50, 52, 54" and so on — all numbers increasing by two. After a few tries, and getting affirmative answers each time, they would become confident that the rule involved numbers increasing by two, without exploring alternative possibilities.

Actually, the rule Wason was looking for is much simpler — it entails numbers merely increasing. Examples of valid sequences could be "1, 2, 3" or "10, 20, 40" or "400, 678, 10,944." And testing such an alternative would be easy. All the subjects would have had to do was offer Wason a sequence like "1, 2, 3" to test it, and it would have been affirmed. Or subjects could have thrown out any series of numbers — for example, "5, 4, 3" — to see if this elicited a positive or negative answer. And that information would have told them a lot about whether their guess about the rule was correct.

The profound discovery Wason made was that most people process the same information over and over until proven wrong, without searching for alternatives, even when there is no penalty for asking questions that give them a negative answer. Incredibly, in his hundreds of experiments, he never had an instance in which someone spontaneously offered an alternative hypothesis to find out if it were true. In short, his subjects didn't even try to find out if there was a simpler, or even another, rule.

THE CATHEDRAL

Before you go to school, your mind is like a cathedral with a long central hall where information enters and intermingles and combines with other information without distinction. Education changes that. Education changes the cathedral of your mind into a long hall with doors on the sides that lead to private rooms segregated from the main assembly.

When information enters the hall, it's recognized, labeled, boxed, and then sent to one of the private rooms and trapped inside. One room is labeled "biology," one room is labeled "electronics," one room is labeled "business," one room is for religion, one is for agriculture, one is for math, and so on. We're taught that, when we need ideas or solutions, we should go to the appropriate room and find the appropriate box and search inside.

We're taught not to mix the contents of the rooms. For example, if you're working on a business problem, go to the business room, and stay out of all the other rooms. If you're working on a medical problem, stay out of the religion room; and if you're an electronics expert, stay out of the agriculture room; and so on. The more education people have, the more private rooms and boxes they have, and the more specialized their expertise becomes — and the more limited their imagination becomes.

I sometimes think this is why the person who knows more, sees less; and the person who knows less, sees more. Maybe this is why it took a child to invent the television. Twelve-year-old Philo Farnsworth was tilling a potato field back and forth with a horse-drawn harrow in Rigby, Idaho, while thinking about what his chemistry teacher had taught him about the electron and electricity. Philo conceptually blended tilling a potato field with the attributes of electronic beams and realized that an electron beam could scan images the same way farmers till a field — row by row — or the same way a person reads a book, line by line. (Interestingly, the first image ever transmitted was a dollar sign.) Amazingly, this was 1921, and a child conceived the idea of television while the mind-sets of thousands of electronic experts prevented them from looking at the same information they had always looked at and seeing something different.

Maybe education's stifling effect on imagination is also why Leonardo da Vinci is considered the greatest genius in all of history.

Leonardo, a polymath, was not allowed to attend a university, because he was born out of wedlock. Because of his lack of a formal education, his mind was like a cathedral with a long hall and no separate rooms. He enjoyed fluidity of thought, as his concepts, thoughts, and ideas intermixed and danced with each other. His mind integrated information instead of segregating it. This is why he was polymathic. He created breakthroughs in art, science, engineering, military science, invention, and medicine.

ANSWER KEY: The puzzle is difficult because we are used to looking at information one way. To solve the problem, you have to change the way you look at it by turning it upside down, with the boxes to the left and the 1 to the right. Then take the rightmost pick from the leftmost box and move it over the 1 to form a *T*. In the middle box, raise the bottom pick to the middle of the box to form an *A*. You now have "CAT."

Rearrange toothpicks upside down:

Then move two toothpicks to make "CAT"

THE SAME OLD IDEAS

*Why do you keep coming up
with the same old ideas
over and over?*

R ead the following:

THOUGHT EXPERIMENT

Aoccdrnig to rscheearch at Cmabrigde Uinervtisy, it deosnt mttaer in waht oredr the litteers in a wrod are. The olny iprmoetnt tihng is taht the frist and lsat ltteer be at the rghit pclae. The rset can be a ttoal mses and you can sitll raed it wouthit a porbelm. Tihs is besauae ocne we laren how to raed we bgien to aargnre the lteerts in our mnid to see waht we epxcet tp see. The huamn mnid deos not raed ervey lteter by istlef, but the wrod as a wlohe. We do tihs ucnsolniuscoy.

Amazing, isn't it? These are jumbled letters, not words, yet our minds see them as words. How is this possible? How do our minds do this?

Think of your mind as a bowl of butter with a surface that is perfectly flat. Imagine gently pouring hot water on the butter from a teaspoon and then gently tipping the bowl so that it runs off. After many repetitions of this process, the surface of the butter will self-organize into ruts, indentations, channels, and grooves.

New water will automatically flow into the existing grooves. After a while, it will take only a tiny bit of water to activate an entire channel.

MENTAL PATTERNS

When information enters the mind, it self-organizes into patterns and ruts much like the hot water on butter. New information automatically flows into the preformed grooves. After a while, the channels become so deep it takes only a bit of information to activate an entire channel. This is the pattern recognition and pattern completion process of the brain. Even if much of the information is out of the channel, the pattern will be activated. The mind automatically corrects and completes the information to select and activate a pattern.

This is why you can read the jumbled letters on page 11 as words. The first and last letters of the words are correct. For example, in the word *According*, I kept the "A" and "g" in place and mixed up the rest into the nonsense word *Aoccdrnig*. Just this tiny bit of information (the first and last letters) is enough to activate the word pattern in your brain, and you read "According."

This is also why, when we sit down and try to will new ideas, new solutions, we tend to keep coming up with the same old ideas. Information is flowing down the same ruts and grooves making the same old connections, producing the same old ideas over and over again. Even tiny bits of information are enough to activate the same patterns over and over again.

How do you spell silk?
Now say silk five times.
silk.
silk.
silk.
silk.
silk.

What do cows drink?

Most people say "milk." It seems so obvious; the word automatically comes to mind. It is, of course, wrong. Cows drink water. Repeating the word *silk* creates a mini thinking pattern. When the question about what cows drink is posed, the pattern automatically establishes the direction in which to approach the problem.

Patterns like this enable us to simplify and cope with a complex world. They give us precision as we perform repetitive tasks, such as driving an automobile, writing a book, teaching a class, or making a sales presentation. Patterns enable us to perform routine tasks rapidly and accurately. When we see something that we have seen before, we understand what it means immediately. We don't have to spend time studying and analyzing it. For example, we automatically know that the logo below represents the Coca-Cola company.

Habits, thinking patterns, and routines with which we approach life gradually accumulate until they significantly reduce our awareness of other possibilities. It's as if a cataract develops over our imagination over time, and its effects only slowly become obvious. The accumulation goes almost unnoticed until the cataract reduces our awareness significantly. Have you noticed, for example, that the logo is not a logo for Coca-Cola? It reads *Coca-Coca*.

YOU CANNOT WILL A NEW IDEA

THOUGHT EXPERIMENT

Try the following test.

1. While sitting at your desk in front of your computer, lift your right foot off the floor and make clockwise circles.
2. Now, while doing this, draw the number *6* in the air with your right hand.
3. Your foot will change direction.

No matter how many times you try this experiment, you cannot prevent your foot from changing direction. It's preprogrammed in your brain.

You cannot will yourself to change your thinking patterns any more than you can stop your foot from changing direction, no matter how inspired you are to do so. You need some means of producing variation in your ideas.

How, then, can we change our thinking patterns? Think again about the dish of butter with all the preformed channels. Creativity occurs when we tilt the bowl of butter in a different direction and force the water (information) to create new channels and make new connections with other channels. These new connections give you different ways to focus your attention and different ways to interpret whatever you are focusing on.

Nature creates variation by means of genetic mutations. Creative thinkers get variation by conceptually combining dissimilar subjects, which changes their thinking patterns and provides them with a variety of alternatives and conjectures.

For example, suppose you want to improve the flashlight. If you sit down and think about flashlights, and will yourself to get ideas, you will likely come up with mostly the usual ideas, and the improvements will be marginal.

However, if you conceptually blend a flashlight with, say, a garage door opener, you will change your thinking patterns, and this will ignite your imagination. Combining a flashlight with a garage door opener gives you a different way to look at a flashlight. This may inspire the idea of a "Superman" flashlight, which is an X-ray flashlight that uses simple microwave technology. The flashlight emits radiation about the same strength as a garage door opener. Like the door sensors, the beam detects motion, including breathing. It can even detect people hiding, by a data display on a screen. You cannot get this kind of idea using your conventional way of thinking.

THOUGHT EXPERIMENT

Below are four pairs of objects. Try to conceptually blend each pair of objects into a new product. Think of the characteristics of each object. Think of similarities and differences. See what you can invent.

Bathtub...Hammock
Sunglasses..Windows
Suntan lotion...Insect repellent
Bicycle...Washing machine

All four of these pairs have resulted in new products. The ideas "bathtub" and "hammock" combined to become a baby tub with a simple hammock in the tub. The hammock has a headrest that holds the baby's head securely, leaving the parent's hands free to do the washing. The ideas "sunglasses" and "windows" combined to form the idea of tinted house windows that, like some tinted sunglasses, are designed to change colors with ultraviolet light. The tinted windows help keep the house cool. "Suntan lotion" and "insect repellent" combined to form a new product — one lotion that protects against both the sun and insects. Combining "bicycle" with "washing machine" created a human-powered washing machine: an exercise bike with a lithium-ion battery that collects energy as you pedal is wired to a front-loading machine. When you pedal, you power the machine. Twenty minutes' effort is said to give you one cold-wash cycle without drawing power from the grid. Think about it. You're exercising and doing the wash simultaneously, while also saving natural resources.

It is the marriage of dissimilar subjects or concepts that excites the imagination — so that it creates different thinking patterns — and produces novel ideas. What would happen if, for example, you combined pizza with cleaning bathroom mirrors in a school?

Peggy Dupra, a middle-school principal, had a problem with female pupils who were experimenting with lipstick. The girls were kissing the mirrors in the bathroom, leaving their lip prints behind. The maintenance department constantly asked her to have the pupils stop. Peggy lectured and pleaded with the girls and threatened them with detention, but nothing seemed to help.

Peggy was familiar with ways of changing her thinking patterns by combining her problem with something totally unrelated. One day she noticed a group of her students sharing a pizza. She decided to combine her bathroom-mirror problem with a pizza. She considered various aspects of pizzas, including:

What can be used as pizza toppings?
Other pizza ingredients
Pizza parties

Pizza chain stores
Pizza slices

Then she reminisced about her personal experiences with pizza. She recalled a local pizza parlor that had been put out of business because of a vicious rumor spread by a vindictive customer. According to the rumor, the pizza parlor was using sewage water from a nearby ditch to make pizzas in order to save water. Though it was untrue, people refused to eat their pizza after that, and this memory inspired Peggy's idea.

After conspiring with the school's janitor, she invited the girls into the bathroom, saying she wanted them to witness the extra work they made for the janitor who had to clean off their lip prints. The janitor came in and stepped into an open toilet stall. He dipped his squeegee into a toilet, shook off the excess water, and then used the squeegee to clean the mirrors. This demonstration solved the problem.

Peggy demonstrated the skill to combine two dissimilar activities to create a novel solution to her problem. The next chapter will show that some of the most creative and innovative people throughout history have been skilled at forcing new connections by means of conceptual blending.

HOW TO THINK LIKE A GENIUS

*Geniuses are geniuses because they form
more novel combinations than the merely talented.*

— DEAN KEITH SIMONTON

Geniuses do not get their breakthrough ideas because they are more intelligent, better educated, or more experienced, or because creativity is genetically determined. Psychologist Dean Keith Simonton observed that creative thinking demands the ability to make novel combinations. If you examine most any idea, you will discover that the majority of ideas are created by combining two or more different elements into something else.

Creative thinkers form more novel combinations because they routinely conceptually blend objects, concepts, and ideas from two different contexts or categories that logical thinkers conventionally consider separate. It is the conceptual blending of dissimilar concepts that leads to original ideas and insights.

In nature, a rich mixture of any two forces will produce patterns. For example, pour water on a flat, polished surface. The water will spread out in a unique pattern of drops. The pattern is created by two forces: gravity and surface tension. Gravity spreads the water, and surface tension causes the water molecules to join together in drops. It is the combination of the two different forces that creates the unique, complex pattern of drops.

Similarly, when two dissimilar subjects are conceptually blended together in the imagination, new complex patterns are formed that create new ideas. The two subjects cross-catalyze each other like two chemicals that both must be present in order for a new concept, product, or idea to form. This strongly resembles the creative process of genetic recombination in nature. Chromosomes exchange genes to create emergent new beings. Think of elements and patterns of ideas as genes that combine and recombine to create new patterns that lead to new ideas.

The new ideas are not only greater than the sums of their parts, but they are *different from* the sums of their parts. The following thought experiment shows how to make a physical model of the process that inspired George de Mestral, a Swiss inventor, to invent a new type of fastener.

THOUGHT EXPERIMENT

1. Take a long rectangular strip of paper. Write "burdock" on one side and "zipper" on the other side.

2. Give the strip a half twist (turn one end over).

3. Tape the ends together.

You have taken a strip of paper with two sides (with *burdock* on one and *zipper* on the other side) and transformed it into a continuous surface with only one side. The two are now one. To prove this, draw a line down the middle of the strip until you get back to your starting point. You will find that you have drawn on both sides of the paper. Similarly, the strip has only one edge. Make a mark with a felt tip highlighter on one point of the edge. Now start at the mark and trace along the edge with the highlighter. You will find that you get to the opposite point on the edge before you get back to the starting point.

You have created a model of a Möbius strip, which was invented in 1858 by the German mathematician August Ferdinand Mobius. The strip represents the process of conceptual blending. You take two discrete subjects that are normally presented as radically distinct, and you blend them into one continuous whole.

In our thought experiment, when you analyze the attributes of a burdock plant and a zipper, you can begin to understand how George de Mestral invented Velcro. He made an abstract analogy between a burr from a burdock plant and a zipper when he examined the small hooks that enabled the seed-bearing burr to cling so tenaciously to the tiny loops in the fabric of his pants. This inspired him to invent a two-sided fastener (two-sided like a zipper), one side with stiff hooks like the burrs and the other side with soft loops like the fabric of his pants.

If George de Mestral had focused on improving the zipper by thinking logically and analytically, he could not have been inspired to invent Velcro. You cannot create something out of nothing. In mathematics, the mathematician Gregory Chaitin proved that no program can generate a number more complex than itself, any more than a one-hundred-pound pregnant woman can birth a two-hundred-pound child. The same principle applies to creative thinking. New ideas are created by combining two or more dissimilar elements.

Conceptual blending creates different thinking patterns. Think for a moment about hydrogen and oxygen. Blend them together in the right proportions and you have something different from either of the gases alone. You have water. Who could have predicted, from knowing about either hydrogen or oxygen alone, that ice would float or a hot shower would feel so good? Simple concepts are like these simple gases. Alone, they have known and obvious properties. Put them together and seemingly magical transformations can occur.

Think for a moment about musical concerts. Concertgoers passively listen to music and politely applaud when the performance is finished. Can you come up with ideas to make a concert a more interactive experience for the audience? List your ideas before you read the following thought experiment.

THOUGHT EXPERIMENT

Now think about how things interact. For example, think about people interacting on the computer, politicians interacting with voters, ships at sea interacting with each other via light signals, teachers interacting with students, fans doing the wave in football stadiums, airport security cameras interacting and analyzing the people boarding planes, and karaoke bars where people interact with the music by singing on stage.

Then think about computers, the football wave, light signals, cameras, and karaoke, and see if you can construct analogical connections between some or all of these and make concert audiences active and interactive with the orchestra.

How did you do? A group of collaborators from the American Composers Orchestra blended the components listed in the experiment into an idea that invites the audience to shape the music an orchestra plays. Each audience member is given a battery-operated light stick, which he or she waves back and forth over the course of the piece. Computer software analyzes live video of the audience and sends instructions to each musician by means of multicolored lights mounted on each player's stand. Imagine the sight of six hundred audience members shaping music with their light sticks for a twenty-five-player chamber orchestra.

When one drop of water is added to another drop, they make only one drop, not two. Anecdotally, when you add one concept to another, they make one concept, not two. Trying to create new ideas for musical orchestras by thinking only of what you know about orchestras will likely not lead to much. But when you combine an orchestra with a variety of dissimilar subjects, you'll find you begin generating novel ideas almost involuntarily.

Consider the fact that you readily understand simple verbal combinations such as "conference call," "home page," "party girl," "finger lakes," and playing the "race card." These are examples of verbal blending; in them, two concepts are blended, consolidated, and articulated as one. "Religious right," for instance, refers to a group of people with strong religious beliefs who try to influence the political process.

Gregory Murphy of the University of Illinois had people rate whether certain properties could be correctly ascribed to individual concepts and their combinations. One set of concepts consisted of the individual words *empty* and *store* and their combination *empty store*. Consider the property "losing money." Like the subjects in Murphy's study, you probably recognize that losing money is typical of "empty stores," but not of "stores" in general or of things that are "empty." Meaning changes when we combine concepts, and the more novel the combination, the more novel the new meaning.

Thinking conceptually about two dissimilar subjects, your mind blends the different concepts for you by recognizing only those abstract patterns of each concept that are interesting based on your unique set of circumstances. These patterns are connected and projected into the blend by your imagination. The blend then bubbles up in the form of ideas and insights. This transcends logical thinking. This is creative thinking.

HOW THE WINE PRESS LED
TO THE INFORMATION AGE

Another classic example that illustrates the process of conceptual blending is the story of Johannes Gutenberg, a German goldsmith who invented a moveable-type printing press and, in so doing, revolutionized the storage and transmission of information. Had he concentrated on what was known about reproducing text and pictures and logically excluded all else, he might have come up with some marginal improvement. Instead he created the information age. How did he get his idea?

Before the printing press, pictures and text were engraved on blocks of wet wood. Then sheets of damp paper covered with a fine dust were laid on the blocks and then rubbed to get an impression. For a long time, Gutenberg experimented with all kinds of processes, trying to find a way that would improve on this cumbersome practice. One day he went on an excursion with some friends to a vineyard during harvesting season. While watching the wine press in operation, he was struck by the fact that, when the black grapes were crushed by the press, they left imprints on the press.

Thinking conceptually, he discovered the similarities in the patterns created by wine presses and the patterns created by engraved blocks of wood. The idea of a printing press emerged out of the blending of the pattern of pressing grapes and the pattern of the then-current process of engraving on blocks of wood. The flash of insight, the "Aha" that came into Gutenberg's consciousness, bubbled up from the blend, seemingly out of nowhere. Gutenberg put it this way: "God has revealed to me the secret that I demanded of him." It was Gutenberg's perception and blending of patterns from two different domains, not his logic, that gave the world the printing press.

We go to school and learn about Albert Einstein and his theories about the universe. We are not taught how he learned to think. We are not taught what his attitude toward life was, what his intentions were, how he spoke, how he determined what to observe in the world, how he behaved with other people, or how he looked at the world.

We're taught that he was simply a genius. We're taught little if anything about his thinking process that he called "combinatory play," which is the conceptual blending of images in the same mental space. We're presented with his idea about "combinatory play" as a product of a genetically superior intellect. Analogically, it's as if we are taught how to measure daily rainfall by the rise of water in a pail, and never realize that the rain arrives in individual drops.

The academic analysis and measurement of creative thinking has altered our concept of creative thinking. Pedants took the simple natural process of conceptual blending and, by fragmenting it into parts (for example, the act of combining objects, combining opposites, combining the thesis and antithesis into a synthesis, combining different domains, combining ideas, or combining a subject with random stimuli), and by giving each part a different name, they produced the illusion that creative thinking entails several different complex processes.

In fact, what the various scholarly theories best illustrate is our almost universal tendency to fragment a subject into separate parts and ignore the dynamic interconnectedness of its parts. Think of these different theories as "waves" in the sea of creativity. Scholars try to understand what creates waves by studying just one wave and ignoring the rest. They ignore the dynamic interconnectedness of all the theories. The result is confusion and paradox, which creates a barrier to understanding what creative thinking is in terms of ordinary thought and language.

WHAT UNDERSTANDING SOMETHING REALLY MEANS

When the Nobel Prize–winning physicist Richard Feynman was a schoolboy, he used the word *inertia* while talking to his father. His father asked him what the word meant, and Richard told him he had learned that the word meant unwilling to move. His father took him outside and put a ball in a wagon, and told him to watch. When he pulled the wagon, the ball rolled to the back of the wagon. And when he suddenly stopped, the ball rolled to the front. His father explained that the general principle is that things that are moving try to keep on moving, and things that are standing still tend to stand still unless you push on them hard. He said this process is called "inertia." To understand what the word means, you have to visualize the process.

There is a difference between knowing the name of something and understanding how it works.

Educators could better help students understand the nature of creative thinking by offering examples of how people actually create. Jake Ritty's invention is another example of conceptually blending two elements from unrelated fields into an insightful solution. In 1879, Jake, a restaurant owner, was traveling by ship to Europe. During the voyage, the passengers took a tour of the ship. In the engine room, Jake was captivated by the machine that recorded the number of times the ship's propeller rotated. What he saw in this machine was the idea of "a machine that counts."

Ritty was thinking inclusively. His goal was to make his work as a restaurant owner easier and more profitable. Looking at his world, he examined it for patterns and for analogies to what he already knew. When he saw in the engine room the machine that counted the number of times a ship's propeller rotated, he asked, "How would the process of mechanically counting something make my restaurant more profitable?" A mental spark jumped from his thinking about the ship to his thinking about his restaurant business when he conceptually combined a machine that counts propeller rotations with counting money.

He was so excited by his insight that he caught the next ship home to work on his invention. Back in Ohio, using the same principles that went into the design of the ship's machine, he made a machine that could add items and record the amounts. This hand-operated machine, which he started using in his restaurant, was the first cash register. Understanding how Jake got his idea is understanding the process of creative thinking.

To say that the lawn mower was invented in the cloth-making industry may sound absurd, but that is precisely where it was invented. Edwin Budding worked in a cloth factory in England in the early part of the nineteenth century. During those days, the surface of the cloth produced by the factory was fuzzy and had to be trimmed smooth. This was done by a machine with revolving blades fixed between rollers.

Budding loved the outdoors and maintained a lawn on his property. What he found tiresome was trimming the grass, which had to be done with a long, heavy handheld tool called a scythe. Making a conceptual connection between trimming the cloth and trimming the lawn, he built a machine with long blades and two wheels. He also attached a shaft to this machine so that one could push it without bending down. And so, in 1831, the first lawn mower was built.

Mixing occupations from unrelated domains energizes your imagination and lets you think of possibilities you would otherwise ignore. A salesperson for a company specializing in LCD products for advertising sat down one day and listed household objects (broom, refrigerator, telephone, lamp, etc.). The salesperson combined each one with an existing LCD product and then, finally, chose one of these pairings and created poetry-generating fridge magnets. Each magnet has an LCD that displays a word selected at random from a three-hundred-word vocabulary. The magnets communicate with each other to make seemingly poetic phrases like: "The wet crows ruffled coherently."

THOUGHT EXPERIMENT

Following is a list of occupations. First think of any three letters — for example, *D, N, R*. Then, from the list of occupations in this exercise, select the three occupations that begin with the letters *D, N,* or *R*. List the attributes and characteristics of all three. Think fluently. List everything that comes to mind, including any associated thoughts. Then try to combine different things associated with the three occupations into a new product. The letters *D, N,* and *R* give you the occupations dentist, newscaster, and restaurant owner.

- *Dentist* might make you think of teeth and toothpaste.
- *Newscaster* might make you think of weather as part of the news.
- *Restaurant owner* might make you think of different foods and flavors.

How can toothpaste, weather, and flavors be combined to inspire a new idea? One idea you might think of is toothpaste that can report the weather as you brush your teeth. This idea is from David Carr of the MIT Media Lab. He is developing a prototype toothpaste that can indicate the weather as you brush. His invention is a toothpaste dispenser connected to a microcomputer that monitors weather data online. The dispenser can be programmed to dispense different flavors to indicate changes in weather. If the weather is colder than the day before, the paste will taste like mint. If the weather is warmer, the paste will taste like cinnamon.

This experiment demands that you stretch your imagination to make multiple associations between different occupations and then randomly combine them into new ideas. Now, think of three more letters and select the occupations related to them, and then try to create a new business service or product.

OCCUPATIONS

Artist	Newscaster
Ballerina	Oncologist
Critic	Poet
Dentist	Quilt maker
Evangelist	Restaurant owner
Figure skater	Surveyor
Gardener	Therapist
Hairdresser	Undertaker
Inventor	Veterinarian
Jockey	Window washer
Kindergarten teacher	Xerox machine operator
Lawyer	Yeast maker
Magazine editor	Zoologist

How are industrial management techniques related to heart bypass surgery? Heart surgeons in Maine, New Hampshire, and Vermont reduced the death rate among their heart bypass patients by one-fourth by incorporating the business management techniques of W. Edwards Deming, a leading industrial consultant. His techniques emphasized teamwork and cooperation over competition. Doctors usually function as individual craftspeople without sharing information. Following Deming's industrial model, they began to operate as teams, visiting and observing each other and sharing information about how they practiced.

Geniuses are geniuses because they make more novel combinations than the rest of us do. As I discuss in the next chapter, this is natural creative thinking that goes back to the first humans. We are all born with this ability, and we all were once creative thinkers — before we were inhibited by education.

THE FIRST IDEA

How did primitive humans create fire,
weapons, tools, art, storytelling, alliances,
gods, and civilization?

The greatest discovery made by humans is the art of making and maintaining fire, which is why I consider it "the first idea." How did early humans figure out how to make fire? Our ancestors saw lightning strike trees during thunderstorms and ignite fires that devoured bushes and trees. They witnessed the sparks flying from those fires and igniting other fires. They felt the heat from fires.

They no doubt also noticed that, when they banged rocks together to make noise to frighten animals, the banging of rocks created sparks. The ancients conceptually blended abstract connections between lightning that struck trees and created sparks and fires; sparks blown by the wind that ignited other fires; the heat of fire; and sparks made by banging rocks. Then, with intuitive guesswork and subtle judgments, they realized that they could create fire themselves with sparks made by banging rocks over wood shavings.

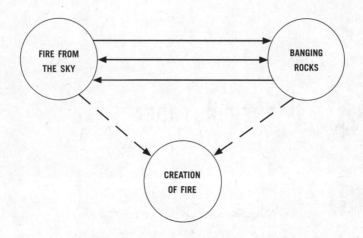

Their minds fused images from different domains into ideas of how to manufacture fire. This is the diametric opposite of logical thinking. It is conceptual blending, in which the thinking processes transcend the artificial constraints of logical thinking. Logic is not concerned with the perception or recognition of similar patterns in multiple dissimilar subjects, which, to the surprise of many, plays the central role in creative thinking.

Our ancient ancestors had no schools to teach them how to think. There were no scientists, artists, philosophers, or doctors to structure their imaginations. Their imaginations were unstructured and pure. They thought the way they were born to think, naturally and spontaneously. They conceptually combined the essences, functions, and patterns they perceived.

Anthropologists speculate that the ancients observed spiders weaving webs to trap insects. Then, by conceptually integrating the idea of spiders weaving and the activities of hunting, they were inspired to weave nets they could use to throw over and trap small prey.

Or consider how our ancestors invented the concept of gift giving. Observing the loyalty they received from their pet animals for feeding them may have inspired the idea of gift giving between distant groups. They conceptually blended "giving" and "receiving" to create the idea of "gift giving" in order to "receive" something. Beads made from egg-shells may have been exchanged in order to secure future favors and alliances when times became tough. What logical mind could conceive of a connection between feeding one's pets and building alliances with one's neighbors?

Imagine how people conceptually combined and integrated bones, stone, and wood with hunting and killing to invent a plethora of weapons and tools. Imagine, too, their blending of visual experiences with cave walls to create pictorial storytelling and art, and their blending of natural phenomena (volcanoes, hurricanes, floods, and so on) with death and destruction to create gods and religions.

EINSTEIN, TOO, CONCEPTUALLY BLENDED
DISSIMILAR CONCEPTS

Albert Einstein thought in terms of conceptually blended essences, functions, and patterns, just as our ancestors did. He did not think with words, logic, or mathematics. He would voluntarily reproduce thoughts as signs, symbols, and images and combine them many different ways in his imagination, which, as I mentioned earlier, he called "combinatory play." How else could Einstein have concluded that space and time are not separate but combined and inseparable? What logic or scientific reasoning would have led him to the insight that the Newtonian assumption that two speeds add up when they are going in the same direction was incorrect, and that nothing can exceed the speed of light?

The same thinking process that led early humans to the discovery of fire led Einstein to his theory of relativity. Einstein imagined an object in motion and at rest at the same time, which logic says is impossible. A man, Einstein thought, who jumps off a house roof and releases any object at the same time will discover that the object will remain, relative to the observer, in a state of rest. This apparent absence of a gravitational field occurs even though gravity causes the observer's accelerating plunge. Einstein's recognition of the pattern of simultaneous motion and rest inspired the insight that led him to the general theory of relativity.

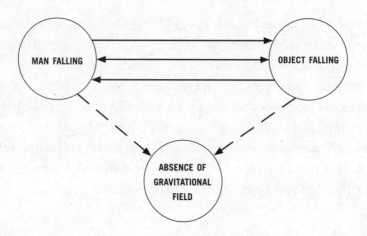

Einstein's perception was far more than the recognition of members of already-established categories — it involved the spontaneous manufacture of new categories. Logic played no part in Einstein's combinatory play.

When you read about the psychologist Sigmund Freud, you find that most accounts attribute his discovery of the Oedipus complex, concerning sexual repression, to his logical intellect. But in fact, logic did not play a major part in his thinking.

It was the death of his father, while the younger Freud was studying the psychology of sexual repression, that inspired his insight. What did this death have to do with Freud's work on sexual repression? It was a Jewish custom for the eldest son to close the father's eyes upon death. Accordingly, Freud closed his father's eyes. He thought a lot about the closing of his father's eyes while simultaneously thinking of his work on sexual repression. He remembered having read the legend of King Oedipus, a man who tore out his own eyes.

Freud made an imaginative connection between the essences of "closing eyes" and of his theories of psychological repression, and conceptually blended them into a new psychological insight. This led to his theory of the repressed sexual fantasy popularly known as the Oedipus complex, which posits that people repress (close their eyes against) sexual impulses toward one parent and hatred toward the other. This insight became the crowning moment in his career.

The thinking processes of both Einstein and Freud demonstrate the subjectivity of perception and how much it is influenced by context. When you perceive intelligently, you always perceive a function, not an object in the physical sense. Early humans perceived the function "burning," Einstein perceived the functions "motion" and "rest," and Freud perceived the function "closing."

PUT THINGS IN CONTEXT

When we perceive subjects as separate events, we imagine ourselves to be objective, when actually we need to become subjective thinkers who look at events in context. For example, what does the following symbol illustrate?

Out of context, it's impossible to know for sure. Once I put it in context with other figures, you are likely to recognize the pattern and identify the symbol as two front-to-front threes. Perceiving the pattern in context, you can easily see that the symbols are formed with the figures 1, 2, 3, 4, 5, and 6, all of which are doubled, one facing forward and one facing backward.

Imagine if early humans had not perceived lightning in the same context as sparks, fire, wood, and stones. No conceptual abstraction could have happened, and fire would have remained, for the time being, a mysterious force. The ancients would have perceived lightning pretty much as a cat does, as something to hide from.

You may have heard the story of Helen Keller. She was blind, deaf, and mute from an early age and could not communicate. Her teacher, Anne Sullivan, realized that the key was to somehow teach her a communicable concept. Sullivan taught her a kind of Morse code with finger play and would scratch the alphabet on her palm to form words. For a long time, Keller could not grasp what this was all about. She said later that she did not know Sullivan was scratching words on her palm; in fact, she did not even know words existed. She would simply imitate the scratches, making her fingers go in a monkeylike fashion.

One day Sullivan, as if in a game, caused Keller to come in contact with water in a wide variety of different forms and contexts, such as water standing still in a pail, water flowing out of a pump, water in a drinking glass, raindrops, a stream, and so on. Each time, Sullivan scratched the word *water* on the palm of Keller's hand.

Suddenly Keller realized that all these different experiences referred to one substance with many aspects, and that it was symbolized by the single collection of letters — the word *water* — scratched on the palm of her hand. This means she organized the many different experiences of water into a pattern of equivalence by blending them with the word *water* that she felt on her hand.

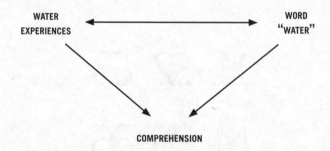

Keller conceptually blended the different experiences with the word *water* by mentally bouncing back and forth and comparing the separate experiences with each other and with the word on her hand. Here we have the undiluted act of conceptual blending, the sudden synthesis of the universe of signs and the universe of things. This discovery of the essence of water initiated a fantastic revolution in Keller's life and the lives of hundreds of others. To further appreciate Keller's achievement, think of how many ages must have passed before humans discovered that a brace of pheasants and a couple of days were both instances of the number 2.

Many people have a fundamentally mechanistic view of the world. They believe the world has rules, and that the rules are knowable. Anything that violates the rules is not possible. For example, we're told the shortest distance between two points is a straight line.

A ⟵————————————⟶ B

Yet if you tear out this page and fold it over, you can place the *B* in the preceding image directly over the *A*, making this the shortest distance. In effect, when you do this you are creating a "wormhole," which is a passage in space-time connecting the separate points. This is the same principle as the wormhole in space that connects widely separated parts of the universe. It's called a wormhole after the hole a worm makes in an apple. The worm could crawl over the surface of the apple to get from A to B, but instead it bores a hole through the center of the apple, creating a shortcut. This violates one of the rules recognized by those who subscribe to the mechanistic view of the world. Yet we see that it can be done.

In contrast to products of mechanistic formulas, the creative product is the result of a process of discovering possibilities in a very large space of possibilities. This large space includes the freedom of thought necessary to conceptually blend dissimilar and even paradoxical subjects into a single entity. An original idea is not the sum of combined thoughts but depends on how their patterns are fitted together.

WHAT IS THE CONNECTION BETWEEN PLAYING A PIANO AND WRITING?

Christopher Sholes, while watching a pianist performing, noted that each key of the piano produces one note. He thought, why not create a "writing machine" in which each key writes one letter? He then went on to arrange a set of keys attached to levers that would strike a roller, creating the first typewriter.

His blend of writing and playing a piano recognized only those counterparts of each concept that were interesting to him as a result of his unique set of circumstances. The blend then released a bubble in his mind, an idea for a writing machine.

The laws of disciplined thinking demand that we stick to a given frame of reference and not change universes. Pianos are musical instruments. A pen is for writing letters. These are two totally different universes. There is no connection between playing a piano and writing with pen and paper. But creative thinkers like Sholes open all the doors of the specialized compartments in their brains — much like our ancient ancestors did — to allow bits of information and thoughts from different universes to freely intermingle and combine.

Think of the similarities between conceptual blending and music. You cannot appreciate the music of the Mormon Tabernacle Choir by listening to its members sing sequentially. You have to listen to the whole group perform together as they coordinate their voices and movements in rhythm with each other.

Similarly, it was not enough for Sholes to think of writing and playing a piano as two separate entities. He had to blend the two together in the same mental space so he could find similarities, differences, and similar differences.

Think of all the wonderful opportunities to combine existing technology with everyday products. An LED (light-emitting diode), for example, emits light when a voltage is applied to it. It is used primarily in electronic devices. Can you think of ways this type of light could be incorporated into household products?

One example is the ingenious combination pillow and sunrise invented by Eoin McNally and Ian Walton. Embedded with a grid of LEDs, the pillow uses nothing but light to wake you up. About forty minutes before your alarm is set to go off, the programmable foam pillow starts glowing, gradually becoming brighter, to simulate a natural sunrise. This helps set your circadian rhythm and ease you into the day. The blend developed an emergent new idea not contained in either of the inputs, the pillow or sunrise.

Or blend a grid of LEDs with a wireless communication platform and have the pillows emit a soft glow when one is touched. Two lovers can be separated by thousands of miles, and when each hugs one pillow the other pillow — thousands of miles away — will respond with a soft glow.

Jacques Hadamard, the brilliant French mathematician who proved the prime number theorem, argued that invention, including mathematical invention, requires the discovery of unusual but fruitful combinations of ideas. To find such combinations, it is necessary to construct and experiment numerous times. It is the conceptual blending of variables from different domains that allows new and exciting ideas to form and emerge.

THOUGHT EXPERIMENT

Among conceptual combinations, the most fertile are often those formed of elements drawn from fields that are far apart. Suppose you want to promote your church by finding ways to help your community. A dating service for singles is remote from churches. List the attributes of dating services, and try to connect those attributes with something that can help the church.

See what you come up with before reading further.

Some useful ideas:

Dating services computerize the wants, desires, and needs of clients and then try to match people who have similar interests. A church could inventory members about their special needs. For example, some members might need transportation to services, or they might need other church members to visit them at home, or might require someone to mow the lawn, clean their gutters, take them grocery shopping, and so on. Next the church could inventory members willing to contribute transportation or time, and then computer-match volunteers with the people who have special needs.

Dating services glamorize their clients by publicizing their successes. A church could glamorize its volunteers by establishing a hall of fame with photographs of the volunteers and short descriptions of what they have done to help others. The church newsletter could also periodically feature stories about volunteers, including testimonials from the people they've helped.

Combining the variables of a dating service with a church promotion forces you to concentrate on "essences" and "functions," such as "matching interests" and "publicizing," instead of labels and categories. In the next chapter, I stress the importance of thinking this way.

5 WHY DIDN'T I THINK OF THAT?

Why do we fail to see the obvious
until it's pointed out to us?

The French artist Henri Matisse argued, in writing about painting portraits, that the character of a human face is seen in the whole and not in the particular, and that, in fact, it may not be captured by particular features at all. The whole captures the essence of a face. To make his point, he drew four self-portraits.

These drawings are remarkable. The features are different in each drawing. In one he has a weak chin, in another a very strong chin. In one he has a huge Roman nose, in another a small pudgy nose. In one the eyes are far apart, and in another they are close together. And yet in each of the four faces, when we look at the whole we see the unmistakable face and character of Henri Matisse.

If we studied the drawings logically, we would separate out the various features (the chins, noses, eyes, glasses, etc.) and compare them for similarities and differences. We would eventually become expert in separating and defining the differences between the noses, chins, eyes, and other features. Our understanding of what the drawings represent would be based on the particulars of the four different sketches, and we could not realize that all four are of the same man.

Robert Dilts, an expert in neurolinguistic programming, has written about another enlightening experiment, one done by Gestalt psychologists with a group of dogs: "The dogs were trained to approach something when shown a white square and avoid it when shown a gray square. When the dogs learned this, the experimenters switched to using a gray square and a black square. The dogs immediately shifted to approaching the object in response to the gray square (which had previously triggered avoidance), and avoiding the object when shown the black square (which had not been conditioned to anything). Presumably, rather than perceive the gray as an absolute stimulus, the dogs were responding to the deeper essence of lighter versus darker as opposed to gray, white or black as being properties." You can train a human to approach something when shown a white square and avoid it when shown a gray square. When the squares are switched to gray and black, the human will still avoid the gray square. Once gray has been defined in our minds, we see the gray as independent and entirely self-contained. This means nothing can interact with it or exert an influence on it. It, in fact, becomes an absolute.

We have lost the sensitivity to deeper relationships, functions, and patterns because we are educated to focus on the particulars of experience as opposed to the universals. We see them as independent parts of an objective reality. For example, if the average person were asked to build automobiles, that person would undoubtedly study how cars are made and then reproduce the same system without looking for alternatives.

WHAT DO PIGS AND CARS HAVE IN COMMON?

When Henry Ford decided to build automobiles, he didn't think of how cars are manufactured. He thought of essences. He looked at "how things are made" and "how things are taken apart." Among his many experiences was his visit to a slaughterhouse, where he watched how workers slaughtered pigs. Conceptually blending the slaughterhouse method of disassembling pigs with assembling cars, he created the concept of the assembly line that made the Model T possible.

The U.S. Postal Service and UPS both worked on the challenge of making overnight deliveries using established systems and theories. They thought logically in terms of packages and points. Say, for instance, that you wanted to connect one hundred markets with one another. With direct point-to-point deliveries, each market would need to ship directly to ninety-nine other markets. Multiply that times one hundred, and you'd be looking at 9,900 direct deliveries. Based on this model, the postal service and UPS concluded that there was no way they could make overnight shipping economically feasible.

Fred Smith did not think in terms of delivering packages within established systems. Instead he perceived the essence of all delivery systems to be "movement." So Smith wondered about the concept of movement, and thought about how things are moved from one place to another. He thought about how information is moved, and how banks move money around the world. Both information systems and banks, he discovered, put all points in a network and connect them through a central hub. He decided to create a delivery system — Federal Express, now known as FedEx — that operates essentially the way information and bank clearinghouses do.

For any individual transaction, going through a central hub would be absurd — it would mean making at least one extra stop. But if you look at the network as a whole, using a central hub is an efficient way to create an enormous number of connections. To connect the same one hundred markets, it would take at most one hundred deliveries. So you're looking at a system that is about one hundred times as efficient. Smith's delivery system is so efficient that the same idea was subsequently employed in, of course, all air cargo delivery systems in the industry.

It is important to realize that the patterns of moving money, information, and goods do not describe an actual idea or fact — they describe the potential for an idea or fact of nature. Banks and delivery systems, for example, are not in themselves phenomena and did not become phenomena until they were observed and conceptually blended into one phenomenon in the mind of Fred Smith.

Following is an experiment involving patterns of numbers. To solve it you have to consider each line of numbers in the context of the other lines of numbers.

THOUGHT EXPERIMENT

Can you discern the pattern and fill in the last row of numbers?

```
1
1  1
2  1
1  2  1  1
1  1  1  2  2  1
3  1  2  2  1  1
1  3  1  1  2  2  2  1
1  1  1  3  2  1  3  2  1  1
?  ?  ?  ?  ?  ?  ?  ?  ?  ?
```

(Answer at end of chapter.)

WHAT DO PHYSICISTS AND DANCERS
HAVE IN COMMON?

The essence of the phenomenon of superconductivity in physics is movement. Physicist Marvin Cohen thought about movement and other processes that involve movement. One that intrigued him was the movement in a choreographed dance. Cohen worked with choreographer David Wood to produce a dance called "Currents," modeled after superconductivity. The dancers came up with some new motions expressing ordered states that provided new insight into the phenomenon.

Their work inspired more collaboration between dancers and scientists. Organizers of a dance festival held at the University of St. Andrews in Scotland invited leading biomedical researchers and experimental dancers to collaborate. The idea for "Dance Sparks" came about when choreographer Tricia Anderson and physiologist Mark Evans mused "about how a dancer would approach complex scientific concepts, and how a scientist might give shape to his scientific insight through movement, light and sound." Conceptually blending the processes of dancing and science has led to exciting new breakthroughs.

Martin Skalski, a professor of engineering at Pratt Institute, is renowned for getting students to conceptualize. Students designing automobiles, for example, might be asked to draw abstract compositions of "things in motion," and then at a later time they might be asked to use the drawings to stimulate their imaginations while designing automobiles. Former students of Skalski worked on streamlining the airplane. Instead of working to improve existing designs, they explored how "things reduce drag." Rather than thinking mechanically about cause and effect, they looked for mutual interactions between objects. The simple golf ball led to their breakthrough idea. They discovered that the dimpled pattern of a golf ball reduces drag efficiently, so the dimpled pattern will soon appear on airplanes.

When you look for mutual interactions between objects, you observe the essence of their spirits. Imagine, for example, you see a rainbow. It seems to be an object made up of colored arcs. If you assumed that the rainbow was an object and walked toward it, you would not find it. Instead, you would find raindrops falling and sunlight. If you study the raindrops and sunlight as separate events, you will never understand the rainbow. But if you study the interrelationship between light and raindrops, you will discover the essence of the rainbow, which is the blending of falling rain and the light refracting off the rain. It's a process, not an object.

How does the flocking and flowing of bacteria resemble the atoms in a magnet? Tamas Vicsek, a physicist at Eotvos University in Budapest, studied rotating colonies of bacteria and discovered they line up like atoms in a magnet. Atoms in a bar of magnetic iron have a remarkable way of self-correcting when some get out of line. The way bacteria and atoms flock and flow will someday lead to new designs for highways and sports stadiums.

WHY DIDN'T I THINK OF THAT?

There is not one operation by which the sun attracts Jupiter, and another by which Jupiter attracts the sun, but one operation by which the sun and Jupiter endeavor to approach each other. What is important is the relationship between Jupiter and the sun. Similarly, creativity comes from observing the relationships between objects, rather than objects themselves, and making abstract analogical connections between them.

You know the "why didn't I think of that?" feeling you get when you observe a new idea or process? We're struck by the obviousness of the idea once we see the analogical connection. Imagine how many entrepreneurs, inventors, and manufacturers kicked themselves when Gillette introduced the disposable razor.

Gillette was founded by King Camp Gillette, who, to make his fortune, pursued the idea of manufacturing something that would be used once a day and then thrown away. He methodically worked through the alphabet, thinking of potential products that started with A, and then B, and so on, listing every possibility. This proved a waste of time. The idea of a safety razor didn't arrive through logical reasoning, but through a moment of insight when he realized that a razor was not an object but a "sharp edge." In that moment, he said, he saw the disposable razor in pictures rather than thought.

In another example, scientists at Gillette wanted to develop a new toothbrush. Instead of focusing on a toothbrush, they focused on "cleaning." Among the things they studied were:

- How are cars cleaned?
- How is hair cleaned?
- How are clothes cleaned?
- How are arteries cleaned?
- How are fingernails cleaned?
- How are waterways cleaned?

They got excited when they studied how cars are cleaned. Cars can be cleaned in a car wash. Car washes use multiple soaping and brushing actions in different directions. The scientists saw a relationship between cars and teeth and incorporated the principle of multiple brushes brushing in different directions into the Oral B electric toothbrush, which became the bestselling toothbrush in the world.

Our special gift is the imagination to make universal metaphorical-analogical connections between two dissimilar areas of experience. For example, in the thought experiment that follows, take the two nonsense words *maluma* and *tuckatee* and match them to the figures A and B. Which one is a "maluma," and which is a "tuckatee"?

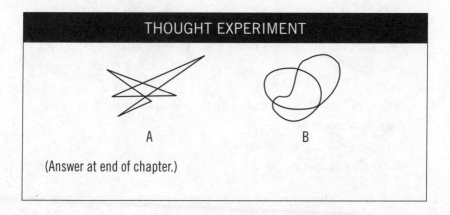

THOUGHT EXPERIMENT

A   B

(Answer at end of chapter.)

Xiaohui Cui at the Oak Ridge National Laboratory in Tennessee came up with an idea to better organize information on the Internet by making the analogical connection between how information flocks and flows on the Internet and how birds of the same species flock and flow together.

His system mimics the ways birds of the same species congregate while flying. He created flocks of virtual "birds." Each bird carries a document, which is assigned a string of numbers. Documents with a lot of similar words have number strings of the same length. A virtual bird will fly only with others of its own "species" or, in this case, documents with number strings of the same length. When a new article appears on the Internet, software scans it for words similar to those in existing articles and then files the document in an existing flock, or creates a new one.

This new web-feed tool will, whenever you go online, automatically update your browser with any new stories added to your favorite websites. It will also provide automatic updates from other websites, such as when new scientific papers are added to journals.

THOUGHT EXPERIMENT

Instead of arresting people who violate automobile speed laws, your city asks you to come up with ideas to make people slow down when approaching a busy intersection. The authorities have already considered all the usual options: traffic police, radar, warning signs, raised crosswalks, and speed bumps.

The essence of the problem is the question "what makes things slow down?"

First list as many observations as you can about how and why things slow down. Some examples:
Tap water slows as you close the tap.
Viruses slow computers.

THOUGHT EXPERIMENT (*CONTINUED*)

People slow down when they see something spectacular or beautiful.
Your heart slows when you're relaxed.
Animals slow down when they are startled.
Football teams slow down when they are way ahead.
Airplanes slow when they put their flaps down.

Before you read further, spend some time and look for cues and other examples from your list on how and why things slow down that you can use to create ideas. See what you can think of.

One town brainstormed for ways to make people slow down. A townsperson remembered the time he slowed down his vehicle when he spotted a beautiful mural on a warehouse while driving through downtown Los Angeles. This inspired the idea to create something beautiful or unusual to slow traffic. His town hired a local artist to paint a giant pothole using a technique (trompe l'oeil) that creates the illusion of three-dimensionality. The giant 3-D painting of a pothole on an intersection works like a charm. Drivers say you see something in the road, so there's a moment of confusion and you automatically slow down. Then you see it's flat and you continue on. Monitors report that vehicle speed has dropped from an average of forty-five miles per hour in a thirty-miles-per-hour zone to an average of twenty-five.

Thinking in terms of essences and principles frees your imagination from the constraints of words, labels, and categories. Imagine you have been raised to believe tomatoes are potatoes and potatoes are tomatoes. And imagine you live in a world where everyone knows the truth about these foods except you. When you think you are eating a potato, you are eating a tomato, and vice versa. Assuming you have a balanced diet overall, your delusion about tomatoes would have no real impact on your life, except for your continuous bickering with others about the true nature of tomatoes and potatoes.

Now suppose all of you are wrong, and what you all think are tomatoes and potatoes are entirely different foods. Let's say they are really oranges and beets. Would it matter? No, it would not. Whether you understand the true nature of your food or not, you still have to eat.

In much the same way, if you are trying to come up with new ways to search for information on the web, and think only in terms of existing search engines, you likely won't accomplish much. However, if you free your imagination from existing categories and think of "searching," and you try to imagine how people and other species search, this might lead you to learn how ants search for food.

What connection can there be between ants and search engines? Rutgers professor Paul Kantor is developing a server for the Department of Defense that will make it possible to find information on the web in much the same way that ants find food by following pheromone (chemical) trails left by other ants. Kantor hopes to enable individuals searching for information on the web to create a kind of "digital information pheromone" path that others seeking the same information can follow.

THOUGHT EXPERIMENT

Ernest Hemingway once wrote a six-word novel on a dare. The novel read, "For sale: baby shoes, never worn." This novel has inspired a host of six-word memoirs that describe the essence of a person's life. Some other examples:

"Never should have bought that ring."
"I still make coffee for two."
"Boy, if I had a hammer."

Think about words that describe the essence of your personal creative-thinking process, and write a six-word description. Two examples are: "Do what is impossible to do!" and "Tombstone won't say: Never made mistakes." Mine is: "At night all cats are gray." What is yours?

BECOME THE PROBLEM

French artist Paul Cézanne, the father of modern painting, changed conventional values of painting in the nineteenth century by insisting that the artist and subject become one. He believed the landscape becomes reflective, human, and that it thinks itself through the painter. By conceptually blending with the landscape, Cézanne said, he became the subjective consciousness of the landscape, and the painting became its objective consciousness.

Blending, or becoming one, with your subject provides unique insights and revelations. Is it possible to conceptually blend yourself with the problem? Can you and the problem become one?

A teaching colleague of Nobel laureate Richard Feynman at Cornell University opened the latter's office door without knocking and found Feynman rolling around the room on the floor, oblivious to his entrance. After he finally got Feynman's attention, he asked what in hell he was doing. Was he sick? Crazy? Feynman said he was imagining what it would be like to be an electron.

Another time, Feynman became intrigued with an experiment in the psychology department that involved rats. The goal was to find out how rats were able to return to a food source. He imagined he was a rat and walked around the room, passing the office door several times. Then suddenly he had his hypothesis. He suggested that one of the cues rats relied on in order to return to a food source was sound. They could tell they'd arrived by the way the floor sounded when they ran over it.

In another example of blending with the subject, a Texas utility company wanted to dramatically reduce its capital equipment costs. Huge power-generating machinery such as turbines, generators, and boilers have a life expectancy of thirty-five years. Replacement of large pieces of equipment like this costs thousands of dollars.

A team of managers imagined they were a kilowatt traveling through the company's various fossil fuel and nuclear power systems. For three months, they imaginatively traveled through each stage of the process. When they began to understand the complex and diverse levels of durability within the system, they took advantage of them. Rather than replacing whole systems, they developed a plan to replace key constituent parts. This redesigned maintenance plan will drive down the company's equipment costs tenfold or more.

Imagine yourself as the subject you are contemplating, or some part of the subject, and try to see the situation from its perspective. This is a favorite technique of T. A. Rich, a famous inventor at General Electric. Suppose you are contemplating installing a swimming pool. Can you imagine yourself as a pool? What perspectives would the pool have about its installation? What recommendations would it make?

THOUGHT EXPERIMENT

Heavy boxes are difficult to move. Sometimes they are dropped, they scuff the walls, and they are generally difficult to handle with care. Metal carts are expensive and are usually not available when you need to move a box.

Imagine you are a cardboard box. What would it be like to be a large box? A small one? How would it feel to be empty? How would it feel to be filled? Filled sloppily? Filled with heavy stuff? What would a heavy box say to you if it could think and talk? What problems would a box have? What recommendations would it offer in order to make transportation of the box easier? How would a box redesign itself?

Take a moment and list your ideas before you read further.

How did you do? Were you able to create ideas for transporting a box more easily, safely, and economically?

One solution created by David Graham, as reported by Yanko Design, is what he calls "The Move-it Kit." The kit includes a set of self-adhesive cardboard wheels and a handle, which can be attached to any box, creating an instant cart. Once home, the whole device (wheels included) can be recycled, or you can peel the wheels and handle off the box to reuse with another box.

Following is one more experiment.

THOUGHT EXPERIMENT

Solar cells convert the sun's energy into electricity. Unfortunately, solar cells waste a lot of the sunlight, primarily because of the material used for each type of cell. The material is sensitive to only a certain segment of the spectrum. This means that light in other color bands is wasted.

Imagine you are a solar cell. Thinking from the perspective of a solar cell, can you eliminate or reduce the amount of wasted sunlight?

Imagining yourself as a solar cell encourages you to think of ways to capture and pass sunlight instead of wasting it. This perspective inspired a graduate student at MIT to figure out how to pass unused sunlight from cell to cell. You assemble many different types of cells, put a reflective filter in front of each one that screens out all the light except the part it can use, and then mount them all together on the inside of a mirrored sphere. Inside the sphere, light bounces around until it gets absorbed by the solar cell that can make use of it.

This chapter has emphasized the importance of looking for patterns between subjects in different domains. What patterns are there between how nature creates new species and humans create ideas?

NATURE'S LESSON

The most creative force is nature. The first thing we learn about nature is its extraordinary productivity. Nature creates a multitude of species through blind trial and error and then lets the process of natural selection decide which species survive. In nature, 95 percent of new species fail and die. Over time, the gene pools for the surviving species stabilize and thrive, but eventually variation must be introduced into them. In nature, a gene pool totally lacking in variation would be unable to adapt to changing circumstances, with consequences that would be fatal to the species' survival. In time the genetically encoded wisdom would convert to foolishness.

Nature creates genetic mutations to provide the variations needed for survival. A genetic mutation is a variation created by a random or chance event that ignores the conventional wisdom contained in parental chromosomes. The process of natural selection determines which variations survive and thrive.

A comparable process operates within us. Every individual has the ability to create ideas based on his or her existing patterns of thinking, which are based on education and experience. But without any provision for variations, ideas eventually stagnate and lose their adaptive advantages. In the end, if you always think the way you've always thought, you'll always get what you've always got. The same old ideas. We cannot will variations in our thinking patterns.

In the next chapter, I'll show you how to create "thought mutations" by blending random, or "chance," subjects or events with your subject. These thought mutations will provide the thinking-pattern variations needed to create novel ideas.

ANSWER KEY: Answer to the thought experiment on p. 44: 3 1 1 3 1 2 1 1 1 3 1 2 2 1

Each line of numbers describes the line above it.
First line: 1
Then 1 1 (one)
Then 2 1 (ones)
Then 1 2 (two), 1 1 (one)
Then 1 1 (one), 1 2 (two), 2 1 (ones)

Answer to the thought experiment on p. 47: The majority of people identify A as a "tuckatee" and B as a "maluma." This is an example of our gift for making universal metaphorical-analogical connections even between words and dissimilar shapes.

LEONARDO DA VINCI'S SECRET

Think like Leonardo da Vinci.

Leonardo da Vinci was the first to write about the importance of introducing random and chance events to produce variation in one's thinking patterns. He suggested that you will find inspiration for marvelous ideas if you look for random subjects to conceptually blend with your challenge. He would gaze at stains on the walls, or ashes of a fire, or shapes of clouds, or patterns in mud, or in similar places. He would imagine seeing trees, battles, landscapes, figures with lively movements, and so on and then excite his mind by conceptually blending his subject with the subjects and events he imagined. Leonardo would occasionally throw a paint-filled sponge against the wall and contemplate the random stains and what they might represent.

Look at the thought experiment that follows. Imagine you are Leonardo for a moment and you see this collection of shapes on the wall. Write down what you think it is.

THOUGHT EXPERIMENT

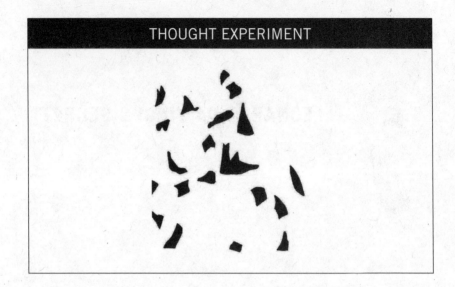

It is nothing but an assortment of scattered irregular shapes. It represents absolutely nothing. Yet some people think they see a rider on a horse. This is your mind trying to make sense out of something that has no sense. Now suppose Leonardo had been thinking of new ways to transport people. Looking at the collection of shapes that I said represent, for some people, a rider and horse, Leonardo might perceive the bottom half to be two wheels. Now it looks like a rider on wheels. Conceptually blending wheels with transportation, he might realize people could be transported on two wheels and a frame that resembles a horse. Hence, the bicycle, which he invented.

Leonardo had almost no book-learning whatsoever. He enjoyed a natural freedom of thought that enabled him to make connections between remote things, including between two totally different systems. He associated the movement of water with the movement of human hair, becoming the first person to illustrate in extraordinary detail the many invisible subtleties of water in motion. His observations led to the discovery of a fact of nature that came to be called the "law of continuity." He was the first person in history to appreciate how air and water were blended together. "In all cases of movement," he wrote, "water has great conformity with air."

Make it a habit to look in different worlds for connections with your subject. For an example of how this can work, take the traditional circus, which, a few decades ago, was in a downward spiral and getting worse every year. A group of young public entertainers (clowns, fire blowers, jugglers, and others) decided to create a festival in Quebec and exchange ideas and talents. The goal was to somehow resurrect and improve the traditional circus. In addition to public entertainers, the festival attracted authors, singers, songwriters, dramatists, and actors. Their diverse skills and talents were incompatible with what the public expected to find in a circus.

This incompatibility of talents provoked the entertainers to invent new thoughts about circuses. Their final idea was to combine all the different performers' talents and appear together under a big top like a traveling circus. They decided to keep the name *circus*, but to change the meaning of the concept (there would be no animals, for example). They combined the arts of the circus, the arts of the street performer, and the arts of the theater into a theatrical show featuring original music and stories in a circuslike atmosphere. They called it the Cirque du Soleil and began presenting different thematic shows throughout the world.

IT IS IMPOSSIBLE NOT TO MAKE CONNECTIONS

The human brain cannot deliberately concentrate on two separate objects or ideas, no matter how dissimilar, no matter how remote, without eventually forming a connection between them. According to his own story, Isaac Newton conceived of universal gravitation when he observed an apple falling and, at the same time, noticed the moon in the sky. These random simultaneous images inspired him to speculate on whether the same laws governed the falling apple and the moon orbiting the earth. This in turn led him to develop the laws of mechanics and establish mathematical analysis and modeling as the principal foundations of science and engineering.

Newton's conceptual combination created new science. The same process can help you to get the ideas you need in the business world. James Lavoie and Joseph Marino, cofounders of Rite-Solutions, did just that when they needed an employee-suggestion system that could harvest ideas from everyone in the company, including engineers, accountants, salespeople, marketing people, and all administrative staff.

They wanted a process that would get their employees to creatively invest in the company. The word *invest* encouraged them to find ways to invest. One association was the New York Stock Exchange.

THOUGHT EXPERIMENT

Your task for this experiment is to create an employee-suggestion system by conceptually combining employee-suggestion systems with the NYSE. See what ideas you can come up with. Suggested tips:

1. First, list the attributes of the NYSE.
2. List all your thoughts about the NYSE. What is it? How do people invest? Why do they invest? How do they monitor their investments? What actions can they take (buy, sell, hold, etc.)? How do companies attract investors? How and why do prices change?
3. What is the architecture of the NYSE? What parts of the stock exchange architecture can you use in order to both interest the company's employees in making proposals for new products and services and reward them for doing so?

Rite-Solutions combined the architecture of the stock exchange with the architecture of an in-house company stock market and created a stock exchange for ideas. The company's internal exchange is called Mutual Fun. In this private exchange, any employee can offer a proposal to create a new product or spin-off, to solve a problem, to acquire new technologies or companies, and so on. These proposals become stocks and are given ticker symbols identifying the proposals.

As reported in the *New York Times*, "Fifty-five stocks are listed on the company's internal stock exchange. Each stock comes with a detailed description — called an expect-us, as opposed to a prospectus — and begins trading at a price of $10. Every employee gets $10,000 in 'opinion money' to allocate among the offerings, and employees signal their enthusiasm by investing in a stock or volunteering to work on the project."

The result has been a resounding success. Among the company's core technologies are pattern-recognition algorithms used in military applications, as well as for electronic gambling systems at casinos. An administrative employee with no technical expertise was fascinated with one of the company's existing technologies and spent time thinking about other ways it could be used. One pathway she explored was education. She proposed that this technology could be used in schools to create an entertaining way for students to learn history or math. She started a stock called Win/Play/Learn (symbol: WPL), which attracted a lot of attention from the company's engineers. They enthusiastically bought her stock and volunteered to work on the idea to turn it into a viable new product, which they did. A brilliant idea from an unlikely source was made possible by the new employee-suggestion system. Just as Isaac Newton got his insight by combining images of a falling apple and the moon, this corporation created an innovative employee-suggestion system by blending the concepts of the New York Stock Exchange and employee suggestions.

The following thought experiment provides a means of producing blind variations in ideas through the use of random words to produce a rich variety of unpredictable ideas. In the appendix, you'll find a list of random words for use with this technique. The words are simple, visual, and connection-rich and will stimulate waves of associations and connections. The words are in groups of five. I suggest you randomly select a group of five and try to use all five words as you do this experiment.

THOUGHT EXPERIMENT

Mark Martinez of Southern California Edison was concerned about the invisibility of energy and its consequences to us. We tend not to pay attention to how much energy we use or waste in our homes. Consider, for a moment, all the rechargers, computers, and other electronic products that are plugged into your home at this moment. Not many of us think about the power grid and the fact that power becomes more expensive to use when the grid nears capacity. And because we are not able to monitor the power grid, we are unaware when it nears capacity. The challenge is to come up with a way to make energy use visible, which would encourage people to conserve energy.

Close your eyes and randomly point to a word on the word list in the appendix.

The random word I will use in this example is *ball*.

List the characteristics. Draw a picture of the word to involve the right hemisphere of your brain, and then list the characteristics of the word. Then think of a variety of things that are associated with your word, and list them separately. Examples:

Characteristics:
Balls come in different sizes and colors.
They are used in sports.
They are a toy made for fun.

Associations:
Keep your eye on the ball.
Playing ball is a good way to interact with people.
Organizations host charity balls.

Connections. Make a forced connection between each "association" and "characteristic" and the challenge you are working on. Ask questions such as:

THOUGHT EXPERIMENT (*CONTINUED*)

How is the fact that a ball comes in different sizes and colors like my
    problem?
What if I made energy conservation a sport?
How can I make energy conservation fun?
What is something that would be common for everyone to look at?
How can I create something that would interact with people all over the globe?
What is it that makes people feel good attending charity balls?

Example. An engineer remembered a charity ball where a large circulat-
ing ball covered with silver squares reflected colors and images all over
the dance floor. The event's organizers created an ambient environment
by also using colored lights: bright red lights for fast dances, and softer
blue, pink, and yellow lighting for slow dances.

Essences. The engineer liked the idea of the ambient environment because
it changed the psychology and mood of the dancers. He was intrigued with
the idea of ambience. He wondered how to create an ambient environment
for energy usage.

He discovered several devices, but the one that intrigued him the most
was a device for overseeing financial portfolios. You could program it to
shine with the color of your choice at whatever level of brightness you
preferred. For example, it might glow with a pale to bright green when
your stocks were going up, or a flickering pink to red when your stocks
were declining.

Conceptually blending the idea of "ball" with the idea of "ambient,"
the engineer got an idea to make energy visible by creating a ball that
changes color when the capacity of the power grid changes. The ball
signals changes in electrical rates by glowing green when the grid is
"underused," or below peak capacity, and red during peak hours, when
customers pay more for power.

Conserving energy would become a game, an enjoyable challenge, complete with quantifiable personal bests. As Clive Thompson wrote, "Imagine if your daily consumption were part of your Facebook page and broadcast to your circle of friends by RSS feed. That would trigger the sentinel effect, where you would pay more attention to conserving energy so you don't look like a moron in front of your friends."

Now think of one of your current challenges or problems. Frame the challenge. Then close your eyes and randomly select one word or a group of five words on the "Random Words" list in the appendix. Follow the same general procedure as outlined in this thought experiment and see what ideas you can create.

THIS IS A NATURAL WAY OF THINKING

Blending concepts is a way of thinking and imagining so natural that we don't even notice how fantastic this ability is. A good example is the ordinary metaphor. If you look at a phrase such as "They are digging their financial grave," you know immediately what is meant. Yet there is no connection whatsoever between digging a grave and investing money. There is no logical way to connect graves and money. How is it possible to know what this means?

Your mind takes one input, "grave digging," and another input, "financial investment," and conceptually blends them together. But the meaning isn't contained in either input; the meaning is constructed in the blend. Through conscious and subconscious elaboration, the blend develops a structure not provided by the inputs to create an emergent new meaning.

How can you connect a coconut, a sensor, and airplane noise? An activist-researcher whose work focuses on the intersections between art, activism, and technology became annoyed at the noise made by aircraft flying over the city he lived in. He constructed a site-specific art installation, *Tripwire*, which responded to the relationship between the airport and downtown. He placed sensors inside coconuts and hung them from trees in several downtown locations to monitor aircraft noise. Detection of excessive aircraft noise causes the sensors to trigger automated telephone calls to the airport's complaint line on behalf of the city's residents and wildlife.

COLLECT INTERESTING STUFF

Max Planck, the creator of quantum theory, made a practice of collecting interesting advertisements, quotes, articles, designs, ideas, questions, cartoons, pictures, doodles, poems, interesting words, and other intriguing items that might stimulate his imagination to trigger ideas by association.

Many creative thinkers have a similar practice of collecting and storing interesting items and using randomly selected items to trigger original ideas. A CEO wanted to come up with an idea to clarify the values and tighten the rules of his organization. He stores his "interesting" stuff in a desk drawer that he calls his "idea drawer." At one point he randomly pulled an article about DNA and a photograph of a nucleic acid from his idea drawer. Then he thought about the characteristics and attributes of DNA, a nucleic acid that carries genetic information in the cell, and made analogies between DNA and a business organization.

His idea was a DNA-like organizational code. Working with his son's science teacher, he created a way to write out the values and goals of the business as a DNA-like organizational code — so tightly compressed that it acts like a mathematical formula. It locks the organization in to prescribed values and rules of action and clearly differentiates it from its competitors. Employees know what the code is and what the rules are, and the company's salespeople proudly display the DNA to prospective clients.

USE PICTURES AND ILLUSTRATIONS
AS RANDOM STIMULI

Pictures, photographs, and illustrations are excellent sources of unrelated stimuli. Select two or three interesting pictures at random that have nothing to do with your problem. Describe one of the pictures in detail. List descriptors — list everything that comes to mind: imagery, feelings, words, phrases, and so on. If you think of absurd material, list that too. Then force yourself to conceptually blend the descriptors with your challenge.

This is what a sales manager for a pharmaceutical company did. She filled one whole office wall with interesting pictures of landscapes, products, people, animals, and symbols. Every time she found something interesting, she tacked it on the wall. One day, she wanted an idea to differentiate her business cards from the competition.

She looked at the pictures on the wall. One was a picture of a rural road through a field of sunflowers, and the other was a sunset over a field of flowers. She wrote every descriptor that came to mind for roads, sunsets, and flowers. One of her descriptors for the field of flowers was "seed." The idea of a "seed" intrigued her, as she thought of a business card as a seed for future business.

Over the next few hours, she simultaneously thought about a seed and business cards, and then conceptually blended the two into an ingenious idea. She had the company's business cards embedded with flower seeds. Once a customer reads the card, he can place it in a glass of water or in the ground, and within a few days it will start to grow. Now the card becomes a flower that constantly reminds the customer of the company. This is the kind of idea you cannot get using the prejudices of logical thinking.

We all have the gift to make associations like these. Psychologists have found that if you put people in a room with a contraption containing lightbulbs wired to blink on and off at random, they will quickly discern what they believe are patterns and will develop theories for predicting which bulb will be next to blink. Our genius as humans is our ability to create elaborate architectures in our imaginations to invent patterns and make new connections.

USE YOUR IMAGINATION

Try using your imagination to find sources for random stimuli. For example, pick a magazine, newspaper, book, picture, the yellow pages, a dictionary, or something else. Close your eyes and stab your finger at a page. Take the noun or picture closest to your finger. Then go to a museum, an art gallery, or a shopping mall and list the objects that interest you. Do the following thought experiment using magazines.

THOUGHT EXPERIMENT

1. Collect five to ten well-illustrated magazines.
2. Determine the number of pages in the various magazines (162, 180, 234, etc.).
3. Randomly choose five different numbers from one to 234 (or whatever the maximum number is for that magazine).
4. Think of these numbers as page numbers, and look up one of these numbers in one magazine (for example, page 44). Place a Post-it on that page if it has an advertisement or picture on it, or, if it doesn't, then place a Post-it on the page closest to it that does have one — one per magazine.
5. Think about how the advertisement or picture relates to your problem, and think of one or two ideas per magazine based on the appearance, image, content, or wording of items in the magazine.

A marketing executive lost his job and was looking for ideas for a new enterprise. He collected five magazines and randomly selected five pictures and ads. His collection was composed of an ad for a website designer, an ad for a telephone system, an article about pay-for-sex phone lines, a photograph of Rush Limbaugh, and a photograph of a deep-sea fisherman. These prompted the following thoughts: making money using the telephone, selling advice à la Limbaugh, using bait much like a fisherman, and using the Internet to advertise. He conceptually blended these into an idea for a new enterprise called SOLVE.

SOLVE provides a new service, in which subscribers sign up to sell their expertise over the phone. They are provided with a 1-888-SOLVE97 phone number and an eight-digit extension that is unique. Calls are automatically forwarded to the subscriber's actual phone number — cell, home, work, or any other number. They set their own hours during which SOLVE will forward calls.

Subscribers decide how much their time is worth ($75 an hour, $30 per call, $15 per fifteen minutes, etc.). Clients' calls are forwarded only when they've prepaid the subscriber's rate. SOLVE takes care of all the billing and payment processing, and it pays the subscribers' fees via direct deposit or check. SOLVE takes a 15 percent commission, with no monthly or setup fees. All the subscribers have to do is market their expertise (many do so on their websites), let people know what they're offering, and give them their dedicated 1-888 phone numbers. SOLVE's subscribers include business consultants, life coaches, legal and tax advisors, writers, psychologists, entrepreneurs, and astrologers. Bits and pieces from unrelated ads and pictures inspired a new enterprise.

Examine the next illustration, and imagine that the figures in A represent characteristics of two unrelated subjects (angles and partial circles). Imagine these figures represent a pattern of information and thoughts. Imagine now for a moment that you conceptually blend these figures in A to create the image in B. You will have created a white equilateral triangle. Although there is no triangle, you perceive one. And while it has the same degree of whiteness as the background, it is perceived as brighter. The triangle emerges from the blending of the two patterns. The patterns are fitted together like words in a sentence. A sentence is not the sum of its parts but depends on the syntactic arrangement. "A dog bites a man" is not the same as "Dog a man bites." Likewise an original idea is not the sum of combined thoughts but depends on how it is interpreted.

A   B

Quantum physicists have long reported that, in the world of the quantum, things appear to exist in a multitude of states. This observation was first made by physicist David Bohm in his book *Quantum Theory*, published in 1951. Since then a host of physicists, including the world-renowned Oxford professor Roger Penrose, have described the multitude of states of probabilities as a wave function until tipped into a definite outcome by interaction with an observer with an act of what physicists call "measurement." An atom, for example, remains an open field of possibilities until forced into some form of interaction with an observer. It is as if an atom or electron wants to explore alternative pathways before collapsing into a settled state. This is just what the creative human mind does. Your thoughts exist in a multitude of different states in your conscious and unconscious, all floating in an open field of possibilities until tipped into a definite direction by being forced into random interactions with other thoughts. This is where "random" stimuli come into play. Then the creative mind samples many paths and outcomes before it conceptually blends interesting thoughts together and then collapses into a coherent state that is your logical stream of thought and produces an idea.

Here's another example of how this works. A designer was walking under an umbrella on a dreary, rainy day. He was thinking about creating new designs for rainwear, rain hats, and umbrellas. He stopped in front of a store that sold musical instruments, which was showcasing a set of drums. Thinking of drums and rain inspired his idea for the musical umbrella.

The musical umbrella features panels connected to the knob on top of the umbrella; these panels make different drum noises when raindrops touch the umbrella. The umbrella cloth contains five different types of waxed fabrics with varying degrees of elasticity to create a range of tones and frequencies, depending on the size and speed of the falling raindrops. The designer's serendipitous pause in front of a musical instrument store provided the random stimulus (drums) that inspired his idea.

THOUGHT WALKS

Take a walk around your home, your neighborhood, or your workplace and the surrounding grounds. Come back with four or five things or objects (or a list of objects) that interested you during your walk — for example, children skipping rope, a pebble, a bag of jelly beans, a drinking fountain, and so on. Study the objects and list their characteristics. Then brainstorm for ideas using the procedures outlined earlier in the random-word thought experiment (see pp. 60–62).

A software engineer wanted to invent a novel wireless device to produce and market. He would aimlessly wander the streets and note things that interested him for no particular reason. One day when he started his walk, the sky was bright blue and the sun was bright. He noticed an umbrella with a transparent cover that he thought was clever. As the day went on, the sky darkened and it rained. He returned to his store drenched. He thought of the sky changing color, the umbrella, and wireless technology, and he conceptually blended them into a new idea. He invented an umbrella with a handle that lets you know the weather forecast by illuminating the handle in different colors. The colored light patterns indicate rain, drizzle, snow, or thunderstorms. The handle automatically receives local weather data from AccuWeather over the wireless.

CATCH-22 IN PUBLISHING

I know an author who used Leonardo's technique in a very sneaky way to get his book published. To avoid any embarrassment, I will not identify the author, his editor, or the publisher. When he contacted publishers to offer them his manuscript, they responded that they would not consider a manuscript unless it was represented by an agent. When he approached publishing agents, he was told that they did not represent anyone who was not published. It was a classic Catch-22.

He tried all the conventional ways to get an agent but was unsuccessful. He had to come up with a way to get a publisher to read his manuscript. He had a deck of tarot cards (fortune-telling cards) that he often used to produce random thoughts and associations. He shuffled his deck, closed his eyes, and pulled out one card. The card he pulled was the "death" card. Intrigued, he began to wonder what connections there were between death and getting a publisher to read his manuscript. What does death have to do with publishing?

He thought of things related to death: the causes, grieving, burials, how animals and birds die, how fish die, rituals, memorial services, the undertakers, decomposition, cultural attitudes, wakes, preparations for burial, epitaphs, gravestones, eulogies, obituaries, and so on. One day he wondered about the essence of death. What does death mean? Then he thought that death means to leave one's friends and loved ones behind. Suddenly, he had an idea.

He went to the library and looked at *Publishers Weekly*, the industry journal. Inside he found a section titled "People on the Move." It described people's movement in the industry, such as "editor X at publishing house A has moved to publishing house E to become editor in chief." He then wrote a letter to the editor in chief of publishing house A:

> Dear Editor in Chief:
> My manuscript that your editor X was so hot for is finally finished. However, I cannot locate editor X. I'm told that he is no longer employed by your company. If you know, please let me know how and where I can contact him so I can deliver my manuscript.

Human nature being what it is, the editor in chief became curious about the manuscript and invited him to submit it to him personally, which he did. The writer is now a published author.

BLENDING PROBLEMS

Thomas Edison's lab was a big barn with worktables set up side by side that held separate projects in progress. He would work on one project for a while and then another. His workshop was designed to allow one project to infect a neighboring one, so that moves made here might also be tried there. This method of working allowed him to consistently rethink the way he saw his projects.

You can use separate notebooks to do, in time, what Edison's workshop did in space. Work on two or more unrelated problems in parallel. When you run into a brick wall with one problem, move to the next. When you come up with ideas or moves that work for one problem, try those ideas or related ideas with the other problem as well. For example, if you're working on a new product design at the office, and you're also working on a fund-raising project for the volunteer fire department, work on both simultaneously.

THE EXQUISITE CORPSE TECHNIQUE

Jackson Pollock and other surrealist artists would gather in a small group and take turns contributing to a sentence any word (noun, verb, adjective, adverb) that occurred to them, without seeing what the others preceding them had written. Then the group would arrange the words in different ways to see how many combinations they could create. The resulting sentence would eventually become a combination of concepts that they would study and interpret in an attempt to get a novel insight or a glimpse of some deeper meaning. They called the technique "the Exquisite Corpse" after a sentence that happened to contain those words.

Try this technique with a group of friends. You will be amazed at how easily you can ignite your imagination by creating unconventional thinking patterns.

Board members of an Alzheimer's organization planned an auction to raise money for their cause. They anticipated hosting an elaborate, sophisticated evening and looked for unusual items they could auction. They tried the "Exquisite Corpse" technique during a brainstorming session. The participants thought about what was discussed, and each one silently wrote on a card one word that occurred to him or her. The group then combined the words into a sentence.

Some of the words they came up with were *people, cruises, creative, furniture, charity, designer, custom, art, thin air,* and *celebrities.* One of the connections was *create — art — thin air.* This triggered the idea of "the sensation of the auction." The outcome was that they sold an idea for an artwork that didn't yet exist. They talked a local conceptual artist into describing an idea for an artwork. The idea was placed in an envelope and auctioned off for seven hundred dollars. Legal ownership was indicated by a typed certificate, which specified that the artwork (composed of ten thousand lines, each ten inches long, covering a wall) would be drawn with a green pencil. The owner would have the right to reproduce this piece as many times as he or she liked.

SELF-ORGANIZING THOUGHTS

Physicists have always been intrigued by how nature produces self-organizing criticality. A common example is a growing sand pile. As grains build up, the pile grows in a predictable way, until suddenly and without warning, it hits a critical point and collapses. These sand avalanches occur spontaneously, and the sizes and timing are impossible to predict, so the system is said to be both critical and self-organizing.

Similarly, when you introduce a random subject and blend it with your challenge in your imagination, it may stimulate a thought that will cause a single brain cell to fire, which may cause its neighbors to fire too, causing a cascade of brain activity that can propagate across small networks of brain cells, much like an avalanche of sand. When your thoughts build up and hit a critical point, they will self-organize into new ideas.

THOUGHT EXPERIMENT

Suppose you are thinking about how people get employment. How do they discover which companies are hiring and what jobs they are filling? Let's say you pick up a newspaper and see an ad for a television game show. Think about game shows, and come up with as many connections as you can between "game shows" and helping someone "get a job."

How did you do? People participate in television game shows to win prizes. One idea you might come up with is an online job referral network that connects job seekers to corporate employees willing to refer them to their companies in return for a fee. This provides an efficient job-search platform for people, and allows job seekers to post their profiles and indicate how much they are willing to pay to be referred for a new job.

The corporate employees can then search for profiles that match openings in their own companies, contact job seekers, and ask for their resumes to submit with referrals. Because most jobs are landed through referrals, the job seekers will have a better chance of interviewing for the referred openings. When a job seeker is interviewed, he or she must escrow the prize (fee) amount for the employee. If the job seeker gets the job, the escrow is released to the referring employee.

THOUGHT EXPERIMENT

Following are some of the more common ways to use randomness to stimulate your imagination.

Random Objects. Select twenty objects at random. You can select any objects: objects at home, objects at work, or objects you might find while walking down the street. Or imagine you are in a technologically oriented science museum, or walking through the Smithsonian Institution, or browsing in an electronics store: make two lists of ten objects each, one on the left side of the paper and one on the right side. Pick one object from the left and combine it with one on the right. Play with the combinations until you find a promising new combination, then refine and elaborate it into a new invention.

Example: One person combined hot sauce with instant-tanning lotion. The combination reminded her of an instant-tanning pump system that allows the user to choose the intensity of the tan. This inspired the idea of a pump-spray hot sauce that the user can change from slightly spicy to fiery hot by turning the cap. Another example of a new product came from the combination of a pacifier and an oral thermometer. The thermometer is disguised as a soothing pacifier that has an orthodontic silicone nipple; it beeps when the reading is complete. It also has a large display with a glowing "fever" alert for faster feedback.

THOUGHT EXPERIMENT (*CONTINUED*)

If you're brainstorming in a group, ask each person to write the name of an object on a Post-it note and tape it to his or her forehead. Then have participants circulate with the others to discover another person who has an object that can result in a new product or invention when conceptually blended with the seeker's object.

One Word. Take a random word, symbol, or picture and write or draw this in the center of a large sheet of paper. Then, using the word or picture as a focus, write around it as many associations as you can jot down in five minutes.

Random Book. Whenever you are working on a problem, pick up a book, any book that has no relation at all to your subject. Read through quickly, looking only for ideas that relate to or are parallel to your subject. So, if you're looking for ways to conserve energy, you might actually find some incredibly innovative ideas in a book about birds. Birds in flight, for example, expend less energy in a V formation; twenty-five birds might enjoy a range increase of 71 percent while flying in formation. Let's say you take that concept and apply that principle to commercial and military flights. This inspires the idea of having commercial jets flock together in V formations for long flights. Engineers are presently working on this concept using available technology.

It doesn't matter what the topic of the book is. When you read it with a chosen focus in mind, ideas will just turn up to serve this focus. I've done it with fiction and nonfiction works alike. Of course this idea doesn't apply only to books or written work. Moreover, the greatest opportunity for innovation usually comes from outside your industry.

Toys. Play with toys to provoke different thinking patterns. Playing with toys as you think makes your thinking visible. A brewery sales manager had his staff build a variety of things using Legos. Some constructed structures, bridges, and signs, while others tried to make physical metaphors between the Legos and selling beer. One salesperson built a helicopter and imagined flying around the country selling beer. This inspired the idea of a beer academy that traveled around the country teaching hotel bartenders how to pour a "perfect" draft beer, an idea that the brewery made happen. They handed out beer diplomas to be hung on the walls of participating bars, and handed out other fun stuff as well. Their beer-academy campaign was the brewery's best campaign ever. The salesperson who came up with the idea said using the toy to metaphorically explain his idea made him feel "carefree," and he no longer worried about looking stupid.

Random Collection. Make a random collection of about fifty small objects and put them in a cardboard or wooden box. Pick out any object. What does it suggest to you? Keep that suggestion, preferably your first thought, in your mind. Look through the objects and connect that suggestion to another object. What new suggestion does this second object offer you? Connect this suggestion with a third object and go on like this until all the objects are connected. As you connect them, take the objects out of the box and place them in line on a table top. Repeat three times with the same objects, but in different orders, while making different connections.

Random Drawing. Randomly select a word. Visualize it. Take it apart in your mind. Then try to combine the various parts with your subject. Sit back, relax. As soon as the mood strikes you, close your eyes and begin drawing on a blank piece of paper. Keep your eyes closed and just draw. The lines can be random scribbles, and you can use as many pieces of paper as you like. Keep on drawing until you feel you are done. When you are finally finished drawing, look at your drawings and notice any images, patterns, objects, places, people, things, words, or ideas. Make as many associations and connections as you can between your drawing and your subject.

THOUGHT EXPERIMENT (*CONTINUED*)

Example: A popular regatta attracted over 250,000 spectators. Advertising space at the event sold at a premium. A small company wanted to advertise its website at the regatta, but the company had only a small advertising budget. Using the random word technique, the company's president drew the word *emergency.* Scribbling and drawing the word in different ways, he made an association between it and stranded people seeking help who were making SOS signals to attract attention. This inspired his idea.

The company hired students from a local community college. Then the president bought custom T-shirts and a coach's whistle. Each T-shirt had a single letter on it that covered almost the entire shirt. The students began to walk through the crowd along the river, when out of nowhere a loud whistle blew. All the college students lined up side by side, and together the letters spelled out the company's web address. They became a human billboard.

After a few minutes, each member of the billboard put on a plain dark T-shirt to cover up the lettered shirt and disappeared into the crowd. Some time later the whistle was blown again and the human billboard formed in a different location. The promotion was a big hit.

Blending Ideas. Collect all your ideas and put them in two columns: column A and column B. Either list them on paper, or write them on cards and put them into two piles or tape them on the wall in two columns. Randomly connect one idea from column A and one idea from column B. Try to combine the two into one idea. See how many viable combinations you can make.

Blending Right-Brainers and Left-Brainers. Divide a group into two teams. Have one team come up with the most fanciful and wishful ideas they can.

THOUGHT EXPERIMENT (*CONTINUED*)

Have the other group come up with practical, logical ideas. Then make two columns, one for the right-brainers and one for the left-brainers. Randomly connect the ideas.

Combining Fixed and Random Elements. Choose a specific element of the problem and name it the "fixed element." Now select a random stimulus via any chosen method and free-associate ways in which these two elements could be combined. You can convey these directly to the problem, or use the two-element combination itself to trigger additional ideas. Now select a new random stimulus, repeat the process with the same "fixed element," and, after several cycles of this, choose a fresh fixed element and repeat the process.

Example: A designer worked on the problem of conserving energy in streetlights. He decided that one of his set elements in the problem was "dimming." He considered ways to dim and when to dim streetlights. Then he randomly selected the word *moon.* The combination was "dimming moon." This inspired the idea of adjusting the light output of streetlights according to the phases of the moon. The streetlights he designed would have light sensors built into them that would be sensitive enough to detect the brightness of the moon, and to dim themselves accordingly.

Integrating Ideas. SIL is a German acronym that means "successive integration of problem elements," and it is a process developed by the Battelle Institute in Frankfurt, Germany. The process involves, first, the silent, individual generation of ideas about a previously stated problem. It differs from most other methods in that ideas are generated by progressively integrating previous ideas.

1. Members of a group silently write ideas individually.
2. Two of the group members each read one of their ideas aloud.

3. The remaining group members try to integrate the ideas into one idea.
4. A third member reads an idea, and the group attempts to integrate it with the one formed in step 3.
5. This process of reading and integrating ideas continues until all the ideas have been read and integrated into one final solution.

Example: A group of food chemists in Taiwan brainstormed various issues concerning food refrigeration. They integrated the ideas as much as they could, and settled on developing a new ink that fades from red to orange to beige to transparent in the presence of oxygen. Varying the thickness of the film on top of a food label allows different sell-by and expiration dates to be programmed.

Three Ideas. A team of corporate trainers who facilitate creative-thinking workshops designed the following exercise to maximize curiosity and encourage cognitive integration of ideas.

Each participant in the exercise writes six ideas on index cards, one idea per card. Cards are collected and shuffled. The group facilitator hands out three of the index cards to each participant (but not the participant's own cards). The remaining cards are placed face up in the front of the room. Each participant may exchange his or her cards with these remaining cards. Then everyone circulates with each other and must exchange at least one card with someone else.

The group is now divided into teams. Each team sorts its idea cards and selects a final three. Participants can replace any of the three with new ideas that may occur to them. Finally, each team prepares a creative presentation designed to sell the three ideas to the larger group.

KNOWING HOW TO SEE

Perception is an active, not a passive, process. You catalyze creative thinking by looking at your subject from many different perspectives. With each new perspective, your understanding deepens and the creative possibilities expand. Leonardo da Vinci called this thinking strategy *saper vedere*, which means "knowing how to see."

In the next chapter, I provide tools and techniques designed to change the way you look at things.

7 CHANGE THE WAY YOU LOOK AT THINGS, AND THE THINGS YOU LOOK AT CHANGE

Do we see things as they are,
or do we see them as we are?

The two images below illustrate the angry and calm sides of the human character. Now, stand the book up and back away from the illustration. This effect will work at different distances for different people, but you should see the two characters swap places. As you come closer to the screen again, they will revert to their original characters.

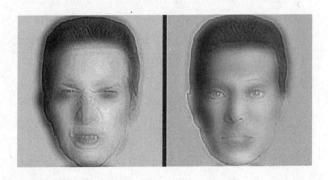

Anger and calmness.

This phenomenon is explained in the work of Dr. Aude Oliva at MIT. When we look at an object, we normally see both fine and coarse detail. However, when we are close by, the fine detail will dominate, and when we are further away we lose the fine detail and see the coarse. By changing the way we look at the illustrations, the illustrations we look at change.

Most people think of perception as a passive process. We think that we see, hear, smell, taste, or feel stimuli that come into contact with our senses. We think that we record what is actually there. Yet scientists and psychologists have proven that perception is demonstrably an active rather than a passive process; it constructs rather than records "reality."

You construct how you choose to see the two faces.

What is the object known as the Grand Canyon? A priest visiting the Grand Canyon might describe it as a magnificent example of God's handiwork on earth. A cowboy would view the canyon as a horrible place to herd cattle. An artist would see it as a marvelous landscape to paint. A geologist would consider the canyon a perfect place to study rock formations. A rock climber would see it as a tremendous personal challenge to climb and overcome. An anthropologist might perceive it as a treasure trove of artifacts from ancient civilizations. A daredevil stuntman might see it as the stage for the greatest stunt ever attempted — a jump over the canyon in a jet-propelled motorcycle. An entrepreneur might view it as a great business opportunity: he might imagine acquiring land and building hotels, restaurants, and nightclubs for tourists. An elementary school teacher might imagine the canyon as an outdoor classroom for lessons about nature and the environment.

As you can see, the perception of the observer depends on the observer's own assumptions. That is not to say we experience totally different things. It's more accurate that we experience different aspects of things. The Hindu's view of a cow in no way corresponds to that of a meatpacker's, or a farmer's, and in Istanbul they keep their pigs in the zoo instead of making them into sausage.

We build our own reality. Even colors are products of our mind.

Vincent van Gogh told his brother he could see twenty-seven differ-ent shades of gray. Who knows if my red is the same as your red? Even if the two most distinguished color experts in the world were asked to dress up Santa Claus, and one were asked to pick the coat and the other the trousers, you can be sure the top would not exactly match the bottom.

An oft-quoted story about Pablo Picasso tells of a time he was hanging around an exhibition of his paintings in Paris. Picasso was approached by a man who asked him why he didn't paint people the way they look. "How do they look?" asked Picasso. The man pulled a photograph of his wife from his wallet and held it out to Picasso, who looked at the picture and said, "She's awfully small, isn't she? And flat." We have to accept the fact that much of what seems real to us is governed by our own perceptions.

WE SEE NO MORE THAN WE EXPECT TO SEE

Our stereotyped notions block clear vision and crowd out imagina-tion. This happens without any alarms sounding, so we never realize it is occurring. Not long ago, a man at a metro station in Washington, DC, started playing a violin. It was a cold January morning. He per-formed six pieces by Bach, playing for about forty-five minutes. Since it was rush hour, thousands of people went through the station.

One man stopped for a few seconds and then hurried. A little later, a woman threw a dollar into the till and, without stopping, continued on her way. The person who paid the most attention was a three-year-old boy. Finally his mother pushed hard and the child continued to walk, turning his head to look at the musician the whole time. Several children did the same. In the forty-five minutes the musician played, only the children, it seemed, wanted to stop and listen.

When he finished playing and silence took over, no one noticed it. No one applauded, nor was there any other apparent recognition. No one knew it at the time, but the violinist was Joshua Bell, a world-renowned, premier musician, and he was playing one of the most intricate pieces ever written with a violin valued at $3.5 million. Two days before the subway performance, Joshua Bell sold out at a theater in Boston, and tickets sold for one hundred dollars or more.

This event, Joshua Bell playing incognito in the metro station, had been organized by the *Washington Post* as part of a social experiment. Because he was playing in a subway station, people assumed he was a street musician playing for handouts and paid no attention to his music. They saw and heard what they expected to see and hear from a street musician.

Thumbs up to the children who recognized they were listening to extraordinary music.

We make instantaneous judgments every day, all predicated on what we see and hear, which is colored by our past experiences. For example, did you notice anything unusual in the above illustration? (Answer at end of chapter.)

It's the same with solving math problems. Our first approach is usually to solve them the way we were taught to solve problems. For example, calculate the sum of the following numbers: 398, 395, 396, 399. If you add them the conventional way in your head, it's difficult to do. Can you think of another, easier approach?

Notice that all the numbers are close to 400. You can restate them in a different way that will allow you to use subtraction: "400 minus 2," "400 minus 5," "400 minus 4," and "400 minus 1." Now it's a snap to see that the total is 1,600 minus 12, which equals 1588. When you take a different view of the problem and restate it in a different way, it becomes easier to arrive at the answer.

PRIMING THE WAY YOU LOOK AT THINGS

I have always been fascinated by how easily we can change the way we look at things. What made psychologist Sigmund Freud famous was not the discovery of a new science about the subconscious, but his representation of the subject in a new way. Freud would reframe something to transform its meaning — that is, put it into a framework or context other than the one it had previously been perceived in. For example, by reframing the unconscious as a part of the self that was infantile, Freud helped his patients prime the way they thought and reacted to their own behavior by framing the way they perceived themselves.

Psychologists Ap Dijksterhuis and Ad van Knippenberg at the University of Nijmegen, the Netherlands, asked half a group of volunteers to carry out a simple mental exercise that involved imagining the mind-set of a typical university professor. The other half imagined a football hooligan. All then had to answer some general-knowledge questions. The professor group got 60 percent of their questions right, while the hooligan group got only 46 percent.

Focusing on the body rather than the mind, John Bargh and his colleagues at New York University asked their volunteers to do a mental task involving words relating to old age, such as *wrinkled*, *gray*, and *bingo*. A second group was shown words unrelated to old age. The researchers then said the experiment was over and secretly recorded the time each participant took to walk down the long hallway to the exit. Those with old age on their minds took significantly longer to walk down the corridor. This experiment seems to prove that just a few moments of thinking time can prime you to perform either better or worse than normal at both mental and physical tasks.

As the following experiment illustrates, you can even lessen pain by changing the way you look at it.

THOUGHT EXPERIMENT

Researchers at Oxford University discovered a way to use inverted binoculars to reduce pain and swelling in wounds. Remarkably, when you look at a wound through the wrong end of a pair of binoculars, your perception of the wound makes it seem much smaller. This perception acts like a painkiller and diminishes pain. According to the researchers, this demonstrates that even basic bodily sensations are modulated by one's perception.

Try this as an experiment. When you are faced with an unwelcome task such as shoveling snow, pruning a hedge, weeding the garden, or washing the pots and pans after a large party, look at the chore through the wrong end of your binoculars. You will be amazed at how your perception changes as a result of looking at the chore in a different way. When you change the way you look at things, the things you look at seem to change.

FIRST IMPRESSIONS

One of the many ways in which the mind attempts to make life easier is by using its first impression of a problem to solve it. This first impression anchors our thought process and biases our thinking. Here is a thought experiment that demonstrates the strength of this anchoring effect.

THOUGHT EXPERIMENT

Following is a set of numbers. Ask someone to estimate, not calculate, the answer within five seconds.

A.
8 x 7 x 6 x 5 x 4 x 3 x 2 x 1

THOUGHT EXPERIMENT (*CONTINUED*)

Here is another set of numbers. Now find another person and ask her to estimate the answer for version B within five seconds.

B.
1 x 2 x 3 x 4 x 5 x 6 x 7 x 8

As you will discover, the second person will give you an answer smaller than the first, and both people will give figures well below the real answer (which is 40,320).

What happens is that the first number of the series biases the person's thinking. This number anchors the person's thought process and unduly influences her estimate. The first series starts with a higher anchor number (8). When researchers carried out an experiment using these two calculations, the average estimate for the first series was 3,200 compared to only 300 for the second. Both estimates are well below the correct answer because both series are made up of small numbers, and this biases people's estimates so that they fall far below the true answer.

In fact, you can bias a person's reasoning by giving her an anchor that has nothing to do with the problem. Ask a person for the last three digits of her telephone number. Add 400 to this number, and then ask, "Do you think Attila the Hun was defeated in Europe before or after X?" (X being the year you got by adding 400 to the telephone number.) Don't say whether she got it right (Attila was defeated in AD 451), and then ask, "In what year would you guess Attila the Hun was defeated?" The answers you get will vary, depending on the initial number you got by adding 400 to the person's telephone number.

Consciously or unconsciously, we are anchored to our first impressions unless we actively change the way we look at the subject.

Chester Carlson invented xerography in 1938. He tried to sell his electronic copier to every major corporation in the United States and was turned down emphatically by every single one. Because carbon paper was so cheap and plentiful, no one, they said, would buy an expensive copy machine. Their thinking process was anchored by their initial impression of the cost of a copier versus the cost of carbon paper. This impression closed off all other lines of thought. It was Xerox, a new corporation, that changed the perception of cost by leasing the machines.

PERCEPTUAL POSITIONS

Imagine that you are on the way to a Broadway play with a pair of tickets that cost one hundred dollars, and you discover you have lost the tickets. Would you pay another one hundred dollars? Now imagine another scenario when you are on your way to the theater to buy tickets. Upon arrival, you realize you have lost one hundred dollars in cash. Would you now buy tickets to the play? Clearly, on an objective basis, the two situations are identical because in both you are one hundred dollars in the hole.

Nevertheless, most people report that they would be more likely to buy tickets if they had lost the money than if they had lost the tickets. The same loss is looked at differently from two different perspectives. The loss of the cash has comparatively little effect on whether one buys tickets. On the other hand, the cost of the lost tickets is viewed as "attending the theater," and one is loath to accept the doubling of the cost of the play.

Our perceptual positions determine how we view things. The actress Shelley Winters was once quoted as saying, "I think on-stage nudity is disgusting, shameful and damaging to all things American. But if I were twenty-two with a great body, it would be artistic, tasteful, patriotic and a progressive religious experience."

One way to shift perception is to try and look at the subject from someone else's perspective. Søren Kierkegaard, a nineteenth-century Danish philosopher, called this kind of thinking the "rotation method." He was thinking of crops while simultaneously thinking about perspective. You can't grow corn indefinitely in the same field; at some point, to refresh the soil, you have to plant hay. Similarly, to grow a different perspective, it's helpful to adopt a different role to expand your creative consciousness.

All of us, with a little thought, can come up with easy ways to change our perspectives by adopting different roles. One gym owner was trying to come up with innovative ways to market his gym. He adopted different roles, including those of a judge, Rosie O'Donnell, a comic, and Pablo Picasso. Picasso got him thinking about artists and their work, which inspired his idea. He hired a freelance caricature artist to sit in front of his gym with a sign offering "free caricatures in five minutes." The artist drew caricatures of the person in a well-developed body, with the gym displayed prominently in the background. The person also got a brochure and business card. His business increased substantially almost overnight.

THOUGHT EXPERIMENT

A hospital is filled with hazards to your health, including myriad infections, missed diagnoses, dosage mistakes, and other complications that arise from human error. And in a hospital, human error seems all but inevitable. How can any one individual, or even any one team of individuals, keep all the tasks straight and anticipate all eventualities 100 percent of the time?

Imagine you've been hired by a hospital to come up with ideas to minimize errors. Assume the role of any of the following:

Priest
Airline pilot
Prison warden
Middle school principal
Football coach

How did you do?

Dr. Peter Pronovost, a critical care specialist at the Johns Hopkins medical center in Baltimore, took the perspective of an airline pilot. He borrowed the concept of the checklist that pilots go through before they take off. In an experiment, Dr. Pronovost used the checklist strategy to attack just one common problem in the intensive care unit: infections in patients with central intravenous lines. The checklist listed the obvious steps that should be taken but were often forgotten.

The checklist was given to nurses in the intensive care unit, and, with the support of the hospital administrators, Pronovost asked the nurses to check off each item when a doctor inserted a central line — and to call out any doctor who cut corners. If doctors didn't follow every step, the nurses had permission from the administration to intervene. The nurses were strict, the doctors toed the line, and within one year the central-line infection rate in the Johns Hopkins intensive care unit had dropped from 11 percent to zero.

MULTIPLICITY OF PERSPECTIVES

Leonardo da Vinci believed that to gain knowledge about the form of a problem, you began by learning how to restructure it in order to see it in many different ways. He felt the first way he looked at a problem was too biased toward his usual way of seeing things. He would restructure his problem by looking at it from one perspective and then moving to another perspective and still another. With each move, his understanding would deepen and he would begin to recognize the essence of the problem. As I mentioned at the end of the preceding chapter, Leonardo called this thinking strategy *saper vedere*, or "knowing how to see."

Imagine three artists who have nothing in common with each other, but who are painting a picture of the same dog. Each picture is painted in a different perspective and style, yet each captures certain things about the essence of a dog. When you synthesize the three paintings, you feel a new consciousness and a deeper understanding of dogs.

How do you describe the illustration below?

The significance of the seventeen triangles arranged with certain regularity depends on how you assemble them in your mind and then see them. You don't look at them passively, but feel the need to give them some kind of meaning and to group them together into a more complex structure. Most people see them as two groups of eight triangles with one in the middle. One group points to the bottom left and the other to the right. The one in the center can belong to either group, because you can point it either left or right. However, you can group the triangles in different ways. You can visualize them all pointing to the right or see them as all pointing to the bottom left. In fact, there is a multitude of different ways you can visualize the triangles.

This illustrates that perception is a constructive, active process, and not just a passive registering of information. It also shows that every act of perception is a subjective and personal experience.

How you see the triangles depends on your point of view. In physics, Albert Einstein suggested, even the distinction between matter and energy depends on a point of view. What was wave from one point of view was particle in another; what was field in one experiment was trajectory in another.

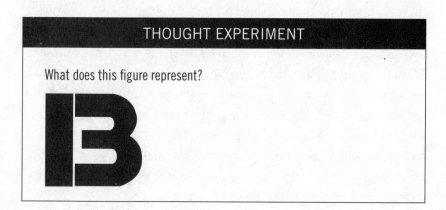

THOUGHT EXPERIMENT

What does this figure represent?

It obviously can be seen as a B or the number 13. The ambiguous image was flashed before volunteers by social psychologist David Dunning of Cornell University, who told them they were participating in a computer game. The game supposedly determined if the volunteers would get a glass of freshly squeezed orange juice or a bad-tasting smoothie. Volunteers who were told that a letter would get them the orange juice saw a B, and those who were told a *number* would get them the juice saw a 13.

Psychological experiments such as this one suggest that our brain is interpreting the world between the eye and our conscious awareness to influence our thinking. Before we even see the world, our brain has interpreted that world so that it lines up with what we want to see and blocks out what we don't want to see. This, some experts suggest, is why experts in any field are always biased toward their own theories and beliefs. They see what they want to see. To reduce bias in your thinking, always look at things in many different ways.

When you use a multiplicity of perspectives, you bring forth a new creative consciousness and expand the possibilities. This is what enabled Einstein to formulate his theory of relativity, which is in essence a description of the interaction between different perspectives. His genius lay in finding a perspective that no one else had taken.

Educational psychologists have conducted many experiments illustrating that having a multiplicity of perspectives opens awareness and creativity. In some ongoing experiments, researchers assign chapters about particular subjects (for example, the passage of the Kansas-Nebraska Act) to two groups. One group is asked to read the passage from multiple perspectives — its own as well as those of the participants — and to wonder what those participants must have felt or thought at the time. The other group is told simply to learn the passage. Invariably, when the groups are tested, the groups that study the passage by using multiple perspectives outperform the other groups — which use "traditional" learning methods — in terms of the information they retain, the content of the essays they write, and creative solutions they propose.

THOUGHT EXPERIMENT

A college must reduce the need for parking on campus because of the lack of space. Look at the problem from different viewpoints — those of the administration, the students, the parents, the faculty, and the community — and then consider the energy crisis as well. Then synthesize the different viewpoints into an idea for reducing the need for parking.

Recently, the administration at Ripon College in Wisconsin faced a similar parking problem. The administrators sat down and looked at the problem from the viewpoints of the students, the parents, the faculty, the administration, and the community, and also considered the energy crisis. They synthesized all the different viewpoints and came up with a novel "free bike" program.

Some two hundred Trek mountain bikes, helmets, and locks were bought and given to freshmen who signed up for the program. Dr. David Joyce, president of the college, said the different perspectives gave them the opportunity to create a solution that is much more than a solution to the parking problem. The bike program changed the transportation culture of the college. The program has been a huge success, and other colleges and universities have begun to emulate Ripon College's program.

In another example, highway engineers were trying to come up with ideas to make roads safer for drivers, especially in icy conditions. They looked at the problem from the perspectives of the drivers, automobile manufacturers, road contractors, road maintenance, weather forecasters, and the highway patrol.

The perspectives of weather forecasters got them thinking about seasonal changes such as rain in spring, sun in summer, changing leaves in autumn, and ice and snow in winter. They were intrigued with the observation that leaves changing colors warn of bad weather coming. Why not have the roads change color to warn of inclement, icy weather?

Researching the possibilities, the engineers discovered a "varnish made of a polymer containing a thermochromic pigment. The same type of coating is used to make bath thermometers and frozen food packaging that responds to temperature change. The normally transparent varnish turns pink when temperatures drop below freezing. When the temperature rises above freezing, the coating becomes colorless again." The solution they implemented was to apply stripes of the varnish to roads. The stripes become pink when the weather is near freezing, and become colorless when the temperature is above freezing.

In yet another example, a group of artists called futurists, who were influenced by the French artist Paul Cézanne and his work, created a new line of artistic inquiry that was based on incorporating a multiplicity of perspectives. The futurists collaborated on a work, with each artist working on it separately at different times. When the picture was finished, they could not tell who had painted what.

The result was a remarkable product that reflected several different points of view combined into something different. Collaboration over time creates a different understanding of a subject.

WHAT IF YOU WERE A BOTTLE OF KETCHUP OR A SALT SHAKER?

Often the key to people's most important insights and ideas can be found when they shift their frames of reference metaphorically. Charles Darwin, for example, thought of evolution metaphorically as a branching tree on which he could trace the rise and fate of various species.

Niels Bohr, the father of quantum mechanics, once said that, one day, he was looking at a friend who had done something wrong, when he realized he could not look at his friend in the "light of love" and in the "light of justice" simultaneously. The two were totally incompatible. Thinking metaphorically, he then went on to speculate that there must be an analogue to this in physics, in which you could not look at the same thing from two different perspectives simultaneously. This insight became the foundation for his discovery of the "principle of complementarity."

It's fun sometimes to think of people metaphorically. For example, many people believe that genes, family, education, and environment have predetermined their destiny. They don't believe change is possible, and they lead what Henry David Thoreau called "lives of quiet desperation."

I metaphorically think of such people as mud puddles. Imagine a mud puddle waking up one morning and thinking, "This is an interesting world. I find myself in this hole, and I find that it fits me perfectly. In fact it fits me so well that it must have been made to have me in it. Everything is fine, and there is no need for me to worry about changing anything." Every day as the sun rises in the sky and the air heats up, the puddle gets smaller and smaller. Yet the puddle frantically hangs on to the notion that everything's going to be all right, because the puddle believes the world was meant to have it in it. The moment the puddle disappears catches it by surprise.

Often the key to an individual's most important insights and ideas can be found when he shifts his frame of reference metaphorically. To see how easy this is to do, try the following exercise, and see if you can discover some new trait or characteristic about yourself.

Which of two objects, a salt shaker or a bottle of ketchup, metaphorically represents you as you are and as you hope to be? Which reflects everything, your weakness and your happiness, your vulnerability and your strength? Forget your likes and dislikes, or whether one of the objects is better designed than the other, or whether one is more aesthetic. Simply look and look until it becomes clear to you which one comes closer to representing you as you are and as you want to be. If you were going to be reborn as one of these two things, which one would you rather become?

There is one more thought experiment in this chapter, one that dates back more than five hundred years.

THOUGHT EXPERIMENT

This experiment follows an idea suggested by Saint Ignatius Loyola. He recommended using your imagination to look back at your life from your deathbed as a basis for making a current decision.

Begin by relaxing in a calm, quiet environment. Then imagine your infancy. Think back to when you were a small, helpless infant born into a particular environment.

Imagine you are now five years old. How does it feel to be five? Can you conjure up images and memories from that time?

After a few minutes, project your imagination back to what you were like when you were twelve. Did you worry? What was important to you? What was your world like? What were your ambitions? What were your friends like? Using the same method of thinking, ask yourself the same questions for ages twenty-five, forty, and sixty-five.

Imagine being very, very old. Imagine looking in the mirror — what do you see? How do you feel about yourself? Who are you? Take a retrospective look at your whole life. What really mattered? What would you have liked to have done differently? Are you ready to die?

Imagine your death. What are your thoughts as you imagine yourself dying? Imagine your closest friends and relatives: What would they be thinking about you? How will they remember you?

Imagine you are going to be reborn. Close your eyes. You can be reborn anywhere at any time, as anything you desire. What would you choose? When you feel ready to open your eyes, gradually look around you as if seeing everything for the first time.

In the next chapter, I'll show you how to change the way you look at things by reversing your perspective and synthesizing opposites and contradictory ideas.

ANSWER KEY:

The hand in the illustration has only four fingers.

8   TICKTOCK OR TOCKTICK

Is the absence of evidence,
evidence of absence?

The ability to imagine opposite, or contradictory, ideas or images existing simultaneously in a conceptual blend suspends thought and allows an intelligence beyond thought to act and create a new form. The swirling of opposites creates the conditions that will permit a new point of view to bubble free in your mind. Imagine, if you will, your pet existing and not existing at the same time. Or, can you imagine your mother existing as a young woman and as an old woman simultaneously?

On the next page is a well-known picture that can be viewed as a young woman wearing a necklace or an old woman bowing her head. Of course, the picture itself is simply made up of lines and dark and light areas. The image of a young or old woman is not really on the paper but instead in your mind. Using your imagination, you can see both the old and the young woman simultaneously.

Einstein, Mozart, Edison, van Gogh, Pasteur, Joseph Conrad, and Picasso all demonstrated the ability to see opposites simultaneously. It was van Gogh who showed, in his painting *Bedroom in Arles*, how one might see two different points of view at the same time. Pablo Picasso achieved his cubist perspective by mentally tearing objects apart and rearranging the elements so as to present them from a dozen points of view simultaneously. His masterpiece *Les Demoiselles d'Avignon* seems to be the first painting in Western art to have been painted from all points of view at once. The viewer who wishes to appreciate it has to reconstruct all the original points of view simultaneously. In other words, you have to treat the subject exactly as Picasso treated it in order to see the beauty of the simultaneity.

Louis Pasteur discovered the principle of immunology by uncovering a paradox. Some infected chickens survived a bout of cholera bacillus. When the infected chickens and some uninfected chickens were inoculated with a virulent new culture, the uninfected chickens died and the infected chickens survived. In seeing the unexpected event of the chickens' survival as a manifestation of a principle, Pasteur needed to formulate the concept that the surviving animals were both diseased and not-diseased at the same time: a previous, undetected infection had kept them free from disease and had protected them from further infection. This paradoxical idea — that disease could function to prevent disease — was the basis for the science of immunology.

But most paradoxes make us feel ambivalent and uncertain, because we're taught to keep opposites separated. We think of shapes such as curves and lines as separate and distinct. We know this because we're taught to know things in relation and in opposition to each other.

AN INFINITE CIRCLE IS A STRAIGHT LINE

Centuries ago, the fifteenth-century mathematician Nicholas of Cusa made the following observation regarding the shape of an infinite circle. The curvature of a circle's circumference decreases as the size of the circle increases. For example, the curvature of the earth's surface is so negligible that it appears flat. The limit of decrease in curvature is a straight line. The curvature of an infinite circle, then, is…a straight line! We arrive at this thought by means of our intellect, which recognizes the coincidence of these two opposites.

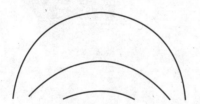

It is the same elsewhere in life. We understand ideas and concepts in terms of their relation and opposition to each other. To get an alternative understanding, reverse an idea and see what new relationships are created. For example, many famous artists have designed and mass-marketed consumer goods such as purses, T-shirts, messenger bags, and so forth for a handsome profit. Unknown artists can't avail themselves of this opportunity, because they are not recognized and no one is buying their art.

A group of artists in San Francisco reversed this formulation in an interesting way. They asked, If the reputation of a famous artist makes commercial sales of consumer goods possible, why can't consumer goods make lesser-known artists famous?

The group holds a variety of gallery shows, and, in addition to paintings, they sell wallets. Each artist prints his or her own design on a dozen wallets, which are priced at twenty-five dollars each. The wallets both produce a profit and serve as promotional items for the lesser-known artists. Wallets were chosen as the medium because they are not hung on a wall but are carried around, exposing the artists to a much wider audience.

Look at it one way, and famous art makes consumer sales possible; look at it another way, and it's consumer sales that make famous art possible. It's much like the illusion below. Look at it one way, it's a rabbit; look at it another way, it's a duck. Either way, it's the same figure.

COMBINING OPPOSITES

Professional inventors love to develop practical new inventions by combining artifacts, using what is called the "inverse heuristic." According to this thinking, if an object performs one function, a new product might be created by combining that object with something that performs an opposite function. The pencil and eraser is one example of this, and also the claw hammer. A small cap for sealing a soda can could be attached to the lever of the pop-top device. Moving the lever beyond the point of opening would drive the seal into the hole.

Before you read further, see how you do with the following experiment.

THOUGHT EXPERIMENT

During flood emergencies, people use shovels to dig into sandpiles, fill the shovel with sand, and then pour the sand into sandbags. Consider the fact that they must both fill the shovel and empty the shovel. Thinking paradoxically about how things *fill* and *empty*, can you invent something that would speed up this process?

How did you do? One idea is to create a shovel with a hollow handle, so that when the shovel is filled with sand and tilted, the sand flows through the handle into the bag.

ALL OPPOSITES ORIGINATE FROM A COMMON CENTER

The principle to remember is that all dualities and opposites are not disjoined but polar. They do not confront each other from afar; they originate in a common center. Ordinary thinking conceals polarity and relativity because it employs terms and terminals, the poles, neglecting what lies in between them. The difference between front and back, to be or not to be, hides their unity and mutuality. For example, "beginning/end" has an intermediate "middle"; "past/future" has "present"; and "love/hate" has "indifference."

Think of the opposition between Israel and Palestine. A speaker at an international seminar about world peace was asked if successful negotiations between Israel and Palestine were possible. He called two young men up to the microphone: a Palestinian and an Israeli. "Imagine you are brothers," he told them. "Your father has passed away, and he has left you an inheritance with three assets," symbolized by three coins, which the monk placed on the podium.

"You are instructed to share the inheritance fairly, but you cannot split any of the assets," the young men were told. "Now you must find a creative solution that will get you the maximum possible benefit."

When the Palestinian said he would take two coins and give the Israeli one, everyone laughed, and the monk said, "Well, okay, but this is how you sow the seeds of conflict." The Israeli said he was actually thinking of taking one coin and giving the Palestinian two. "Evidently," the monk guessed, "you feel it's worth the gamble to invest in your adversary and hope to benefit from it in the future." The young men sat down.

Next, the monk asked two young women (again one was Israeli, the other Palestinian) to repeat the exercise. "I would keep one coin and give her two," said the young Israeli, "on the condition that she donate her second one to a charity, maybe a children's hospital." "Good," said the monk, and asked the Palestinian woman if she agreed. The young Palestinian said, "I would keep one for myself and give one to her, and say that we should invest the third one together." The entire audience stood and applauded this solution.

This exercise demonstrated to the audience that the nationalistic opposites are not disjoined but polar. They do not confront each other from afar; they originate in a common center. Here the participants in the exercise found the solution at the common center. Instead of looking for reasons why two points of view are different, scientists look for reasons why the two points of view may be compatible.

In art, Andy Warhol's genius lay in juxtaposing two traditionally opposite orientations within a single painting. Producing serious paintings of Campbell's soup cans, he created confusion: gazing at them, viewers experience the banal and the sublime at once. Warhol succeeded in combining opposites without reducing their intrinsic qualities.

The British artist Paul Curtis has created "reverse graffiti" that he calls "clean tagging" or "grime writing." Using industrial scrubbers, he selectively scrubs dirty, derelict city property (tunnel walls, sidewalks) so that words and images are formed by the cleaned sections. He calls this refacing, not defacing. His art is temporary. It glows and twinkles and, over time, fades away. He also sells his art as advertising. The London city council has accused him of breaking the law, but can't figure out what law he's breaking. Cleaning dirty walls without a permit?

CAN WE EMBALM LIVE THINGS TO PRESERVE THEM?

Think for a moment about embalming, a process used to preserve the bodies of the dead. The opposite of death is life. Can embalming be used to preserve live things as well as dead things? This is the paradox researchers at the University of Zaragoza, in Spain, decided to explore. Researching different methods of embalming, they discovered that cinnamon was used by ancient Egyptian embalmers to preserve the dead. At first, the researchers believed that the spice was used to mask the odor of decay.

Experimenting with cinnamon, they discovered that, in addition to having a sweet, woody aroma, the spice killed microbes. Spanish researchers took advantage of that property to develop an anti-mold waxed-paper wrapper. They report that, even when wrapped around bread deliberately tainted with mold, a waxed paper made with 6 percent cinnamon oil inhibited the growth of mold by 96 percent, prolonging freshness by up to ten days. (Plain waxed paper did not slow the mold at all.) In addition, the wrapper may also prove effective in keeping fruits, vegetables, and meats fresh. The researchers said the cinnamon waxed paper was safe and environmentally friendly.

Metal parts forged in a foundry can be cleaned by sandblasting them. Unfortunately, though, the sand gets into small cavities in the metal, and cleaning it out is time-consuming and expensive. The paradox here is that the particles must be hard in order to clean the metal parts, and at the same time "not hard" in order to be easily removed. Engineers who worked in one foundry recognized that an ideal substitute for the sand would be a material characterized by "disappearing hardness." This got the engineers to thinking about things that are hard and which disappear. The synthesis of the two concepts led the engineers to think of ice: it's hard, but it disappears when it melts. The unique feature is that it melts. The solution to the foundry's problem was to blast the metal parts with particles of dry ice: they clean the parts and later turn into gas and evaporate.

THOUGHT EXPERIMENT

Two antagonistic concepts are "making money" and "doing social good." Following is a blueprint of one example. See if you can create another.

Problem: How to integrate business with social activism.

Paradox: The business and social-activist sectors of society are separate and have different goals. The business sector seeks profits. The social-activist sector seeks social good. The paradox: a business can make a profit while accomplishing a social good.

Synthesis: Summarize the problem in a few words that capture the essence and paradox of the problem. This synthesis should be two to five words. Some examples of summarized paradoxes are:

Sales target — Focused Desire
Different-level employees — Balanced Confusion
Seasonal sales cycles — Connected Pauses
Birth control — Dependable Intermittency
Nature — Rational Impetuousness

Reducing the paradox to a two-word "book title" makes it easier to work with and comprehend.

Example: In our example, the synthesis is "Social Entrepreneurship."

Analogue: Find an analogue that reflects the essence of the paradox. Think of as many analogues as you can, and select the most suitable.

Example: The analogue selected for our example is the Jesuit religious order of the Catholic Church. This order is a truly effective, global service organization.

Unique feature: What is the unique feature or activity of the analogue? Creative ideas often involve taking unique features of one subject and applying them to another.

THOUGHT EXPERIMENT (*CONTINUED*)

Example: Jesuits have a hybrid-value chain, which means they integrate work for the church with work for the people. When they find an innovative solution for a problem in one part of the world, they apply it to problems in another.

Equivalent: The equivalent of this unique feature might be the integration of social activism and business. Use an equivalent of the unique feature to trigger new ideas. Business would be the "church," and social activism would be "work for the people" — in effect, a hybrid-value chain between global partnerships involving social entrepreneurs and businesses.

Build into a new idea: Create an organization that combines an idea for social good with making a profit, and package the idea in a way that takes it from local to global in reach.

One example was reported in *Fast Company* magazine. Cemex, the big Mexican cement producer, created a plan to encourage families in urban slums to save money in order to buy cement for building home additions, and it provides them with discounted engineering services. Community activists love the scheme because it may help to alleviate family abuse that can come from overcrowding. And in principle it's great for Cemex, because it creates a new market.

The next step is to partner Cemex with AIDS activists, who have established a network that provides sex education and AIDS-prevention training in Mexico. The strategy calls for Cemex to use the AIDS activists' existing distribution system, paying commissions to safe-sex educators when they refer cement customers. The partnership allows the activists to increase the quality of life for many people while creating a new way to generate money for their own projects. Finally, Cemex plans to connect with similar social activist networks to distribute cement across Mexico and in South America.

Conceptually blending profits and social work in the same mental space created a new way to look at business.

Another example of making money while doing a social good comes from India. One family-owned, nonprofit organization in India hired the poorest of the poor, called "rag pickers," to collect litter from the streets of Delhi and recycle it in return for food. This was a social good, but the family wondered if it would be possible to somehow make a profit from the litter and become a self-sustaining nonprofit, instead of depending on the charity of others.

The family worked with designers to create an ingenious product — wallets made from the recycled bags and newspapers collected from the streets. The wallet has the perfect amount of space for all the essentials, and it features an attractive minimalist design. Each wallet — made from colored ads, cartoons, headline news pages, sports pages, and classifieds — is one of a kind in its pattern and style.

Production of this wallet helps reduce waste in Delhi while, at the same time, providing employment and subsidizing health care and education for the poor. The nonprofit organization generated profits by doing a social good, and then used the profits to perform more social work. In a sense, it became, paradoxically, a "profitable" nonprofit.

SLOWER IS FASTER

Dirk Helbing, a physicist at the Swiss Federal Institute of Technology in Zurich, discovered while studying the movement of people and systems that, paradoxically, slower is faster when a crowd of people tries to exit a room through a doorway. An obstacle placed in front of an open door enables people to get out faster because it helps to maintain the fluidity of the crowd. What makes it work is that crowds adjust to conditions. When two streams of people meet, they organize so that one person from one group goes out first, and then a person from the other goes out. The physicist observed that the crowd organizes itself in much the same way as fluids and gases do when forced into queues in laboratory experiments.

Paradoxical thinking is becoming more and more common in the world of science. The world of subatomic physics is filled with para-doxes, seeming contradictions held at the same time. Science, as you know, has two theories of light: one is that light is a corpuscle, and the other is that light is a wave. In developing an equation or an experiment, scientists sometimes employ the corpuscular theory; at other times, they employ the wave theory. Both are true operationally, yet logically they are incompatible with each other.

Another example of paradoxical thinking is from the world of medicine. As reported in *Time* magazine, Dr. Randas Batista in Curitiba, Brazil, had many patients dying of congestive heart failure, which causes the heart to weaken and enlarge. When the heart becomes weakened, it tries to compensate by stretching its muscles to help it beat. But as the heart's muscular left ventricle enlarges, it becomes less efficient at pumping blood through the body. Dr. Batista lacked the resources necessary for the standard American treatments for the disease, which are drug therapy and heart transplant. He came up with a radical solution. His solution was to cut off pieces of the heart to make it smaller and, at the same time, stronger.

His solution — cutting away part of the heart to make it stronger — is paradoxical. Surgeons around the world were amazed. Their perspective had been so prejudiced by conventional thinking about congestive heart failure that they never considered radical solutions until after Dr. Batista devised this stunning treatment. It was difficult for them to think beyond what they had learned.

Dr. Batista's thinking was extreme. Following is a thought experiment that entails combining elements of extreme ideas.

THOUGHT EXPERIMENT

Create two opposite extreme ideas. For instance, consider first what idea you would create if you had all the resources (people, money, time, etc.) in the world. Then ask yourself what idea you would create if you had no resources. And then try to combine the two into something practical. Also, make a list of the characteristics of each extreme idea, and make random connections between the two lists.

Suppose, for example, you want to reward employees for ideas that increase productivity. One extreme would be to award each employee $1 million for each idea. The other extreme would be to award each employee a penny. Can you combine the two extremes into a practical idea?

You might combine the two extremes into a "Penny for Your Ideas" campaign. Buy a gum ball machine, fill it with colored gum balls, and place it in your office. For every idea (or every five or ten ideas), award the contributor a penny for use in the machine. Award a cash prize according to the color of the gum ball that comes out — for example, two dollars for green, five dollars for yellow, one hundred dollars for red, and so on.

A PRODUCT THAT IS NOT A DRUG
YET WORKS LIKE A DRUG

I came across this story recently when browsing the Internet: "A few years ago I was in Phoenixville, Pennsylvania, a small town with many buildings left vacant when the steel industry declined. But one abandoned factory was doing a tremendous business. Their product? Placebos. For almost any drug on the market, they produce an inert replica: round pink pills, triangular red ones, blue ovals, yellow tablets — the entire range. Drug companies have built research lab after research lab while developing new products. Ironically, the placebos are made in a former abandoned factory with no research labs (and no lawyers) because they have one product, no side effects, and no patents." For many people, a placebo works like the drug that it is intended to replace. Imagine the elegance of the paradox. Something that is not a drug works like a drug if people believe it is the prescribed drug. Placebos work remarkably well. Exactly how and why they work is still a mystery.

Think about the business paradox that Kenneth Thompson suggested might be stated this way: "the best control comes from not controlling." Thompson provides this example:

> The legendary founder of Wal-Mart, Sam Walton, was a living demonstration of this contradiction. Walton was normally in his office only on Friday and Saturday, from the opening bell to noon. Yet Wal-Mart was considered one of the more tightly managed organizations in the retail industry.
>
> Someone once asked Walton how he could possibly run Wal-Mart when he was out of the office much of the time. He responded by saying simply that this was the only way to run a customer-focused organization. He spent Monday through Thursday in the field interacting directly with customers and employees and seeing what the competition was up to. In fact, while he was alive, Wal-Mart stores were built without an office for the store manager for the same reason. The manager's job was to be out with the customers and employees.

MICHELANGELO'S PARADOX

Many times we have to change our psychology to understand certain phenomena. Think of Michelangelo when he sculpted what may be the world's most famous sculpture, *David*. He did not think of "building" something; he thought of "taking away" something from what was there. A quotation often attributed to him has it that "the more the marble wastes away, the more the sculpture grows."

To understand a mirror you have to change your psychology. Why does a mirror seem to invert left and right but not top and bottom? That is, when you hold an open book up to a mirror, why are the letters of the text backward but not upside down, and why is your left hand the double's right and your right the double's left?

When we look into a mirror we imagine ourselves reversed left to right, as if we had walked around behind a pane of glass to look through it. This conventional perspective is why we cannot explain what is happening with a mirror. To understand a mirror's image, you have to psychologically reverse the way you perceive your image. Imagine your nose and the back of your head reversed, through the mirror. You have to imagine yourself reversed, "squashed" back to front. Stand in front of the mirror with one hand pointing east and the other west. Wave the east hand. The mirror image waves its east hand. Its west hand lies to the west. Its head is up and the feet are down. Once you look at a mirror with this perspective, you gain an understanding about the axis of the mirror, which is the imaginary line on a mirror about which a body rotates.

We have difficulty understanding the mirror until we change our perspective. Similarly, we sometimes have difficulty coming up with ideas until we change our psychology. Early nomadic societies were all based on the principle of "getting to the water." Only when they reversed this to "how can we get the water to come to us" did civilization begin to flourish.

An easy way to change your thinking patterns when faced with a problem is to first list all your assumptions about the problem. Then reverse your assumptions and try to make the reversals work.

Following is a thought experiment about reversing a store policy. After you read the problem, try to come up with ideas before you read further.

THOUGHT EXPERIMENT

A clothing retailer is concerned about the rate of garment returns. According to the store policy, a customer who returns a garment must receive a cash refund. Reverse this policy so that it says: if a customer returns a garment, the store doesn't have to give a cash refund.

Can you come up with ideas to make this reversal into a practical solution?

What can the store give the customer instead of a refund? One idea is to offer the customer a gift certificate worth 110 percent of the original purchase price. In effect this gives the customer a 10 percent reward for returning the unwanted garment.

The policy would allow the store to keep most of the cash, and the customers would likely be happy with the reward. The real payback would occur when the customer returned with the gift certificate. A customer who returned a $100 garment would receive a gift certificate for $110. Psychology predicts that, when the customer returns to the store, he will go to the higher priced garments. For example, instead of shopping for a $100 garment, he will be attracted to the $200 garments because, in his mind, it would "cost" him only $90. What a deal!

In this chapter, I showed how to change the way you look at things by reversing them and looking at the other side. In the next chapter, I will provide another way of looking at things by imagining the absurd and the fantastical to break up your conventional thinking patterns.

THINKING THE UNTHINKABLE

If your idea is not at first absurd,
there is no hope for it.

— EINSTEIN

Ask a friend to imagine a creature living on a planet with a different atmosphere, in another solar system. Then ask your friend to draw a picture of the creature. Most people draw creatures that resemble life as we understand it, namely, creatures with sense organs to see, hear, and smell, and arms and legs with bilateral symmetry. They do this even though they're free to imagine anything they wish, without constraints.

What they're exhibiting is a phenomenon called structured imagination. Even when we use our imaginations to develop new ideas, our ideas are heavily structured in highly predictable ways, according to existing concepts, categories, and stereotypes. This is true whether we are inventors, artists, writers, scientists, designers, businesspeople, or someone simply fantasizing about a better life.

Research shows that we call up typical instances of a concept faster than less typical ones. To see this for yourself, quickly name the first five birds you can think of. Your list is likely to be populated with typical birds, such as robins, blue jays, and sparrows, and less likely to contain unusual birds, such as pelicans, ostriches, and penguins.

Because more typical instances of a concept spring to mind first, we naturally tend to seize on them as starting points when developing new ideas. And because the most typical members of a category are the ones that have all of its central properties, this can reduce innovation even further. A good example of this is the railroad track.

One summer I worked for the railroad to help pay my way through college. We replaced worn rails with new ones. The width between two rails is 4 feet 8.5 inches. I asked the boss about this odd measurement, and he told me that it had been reasoned out by master thinkers at the home office. He said that engineers and physicists who studied this aspect of railroad building had concluded that 4 feet 8.5 inches was the perfect width.

Years later, I read stories from different sources about the early rails. Most of the stories started with the history of the first long-distance roads in England. The stories confirmed that the first long-distance roads there were built by the Romans after they conquered Britain. Consequently, the Roman war chariots made the first ruts in the roads. The chariots were made in Rome, and the width between the wheels of every chariot was 4 feet 8.5 inches, which is just wide enough to accommodate two horses' behinds. After that, wagon makers in Britain used this same width for the wheels on their wagons, otherwise wagons would break apart due to the deep ruts.

So one might say that the standard railroad gauge in the United States — 4 feet 8.5 inches — can be traced back to the original specifications for the Roman war chariot. The next time you are handed an odd specification and wonder what horse's ass came up with it, you might be closer to the truth than you think.

We need ways to unstructure our imaginations to explore the outer limits and dazzling variety of our concepts, so that we can go beyond the typical and concoct wonderfully unusual ideas. Doing so may involve visiting seemingly unrelated topics or concepts, which may appear foreign and even hostile to the problem at hand. But time after time, this way of cracking the problem code has been successful. All invention and discovery is permeated by the idea of thinking the unthinkable.

IS YOUR IDEA CRAZY ENOUGH?

The playful openness of creative geniuses is what allows them to explore unthinkable ideas. Once Wolfgang Pauli, the discoverer of electron spin, was presenting a new theory of elementary particles before a professional audience. An extended discussion followed. Niels Bohr summarized it for Pauli's benefit by saying that everyone had agreed his theory was crazy. The question that divided them, he claimed, was whether it was crazy enough to have a chance of being correct. Bohr said his own feeling was that it wasn't crazy enough.

Logic hides in Bohr's illogic. In genius, there is a tolerance for unpredictable avenues of thought. The result of unpredictable thinking may be just what is needed to shift the context and lead to a new perspective.

THOUGHT EXPERIMENT

A manufacturer of detergent wants a new marketing campaign. An agency comes up with a bizarre idea: if you unknowingly purchase one of fifty selected boxes of detergent, then when you return home with your purchase, gifts will suddenly materialize in your home out of nowhere.

Can you take this bizarre idea and imagine how it could become a realistic campaign?

How did you do? Here is what one marketing agency did. As reported on PSFK.com, it persuaded the "Unilever corporation to place GPS devices in selected boxes of its Omo brand detergent in Brazil. This enabled the agency to track the purchasers right to their doorsteps and surprise them with gifts. As soon as any one of the fifty Omo boxes bearing GPS devices was removed from the store shelf, one of its teams swooped into action and reached the shopper's home within hours."

The playful freedom that accompanies a "bizarre" idea permitted the agency to juxtapose possibilities that would not otherwise have been available, and to construct a sequence of events that would otherwise not have been constructed.

In another example, Spencer Silver, a 3M chemist who liked to play around with chemicals, tried mixing together different ones just to see what would happen. One of the things that happened was his invention of the special adhesive that made Post-it notes possible, a product that had accounted for over $300 million in business by 2002.

Spencer Silver is quoted as saying, "If I had thought about it, I wouldn't have done the experiment. The literature was full of examples that said you can't do this." If he had studied the literature, he would have stopped his work. The key was not knowing what the experts believed, and experimenting to see what he could do. Silver, in a "Eureka" moment, realized he had developed an adhesive that created an impermanent bond.

But the problem was how to use his discovery. The company climate permitted Silver to continue with his efforts, but no one could develop it into a useful product. Silver had found a solution, but he hadn't found a problem to solve it with. The breakthrough came when another 3M employee, Arthur Fry, got his inspiration. Art was a member of a church choir and used paper slips as bookmarks in the songbooks to identify the songs to be sung. Sometimes the paper would fly off and create problems. The idea of using Silver's adhesive to make a better bookmark came to him while singing in the choir.

The bookmark inspired him to think of other paper-to-paper applications in which only one of the sheets of paper was coated with the glue. The problem was that 3M did not have the equipment to do this, so management was not enthusiastic about Fry's application. Consequently Fry designed and built his own machine in his basement to manufacture the forerunner of the Post-it note. The machine was too large to get through his basement door, so he blasted a hole in the wall to get the machine to 3M. He then demonstrated the machine to management, engineers, salespeople, and production managers. His demonstration generated the enthusiasm to get management behind the project.

THINKING OUTSIDE YOUR CONE OF EXPECTATIONS

Thought is a process of fitting new situations into existing slots and pigeonholes in the mind. Just as you cannot put a physical thing into more than one physical pigeonhole at once, the processes of thought prevent you from putting a mental construct into more than one mental category at once. This is because the mind has a basic intolerance for ambiguity, and its first function is to reduce the complexity of its experiences.

When you come up with crazy or fantastical ideas, you step outside your cone of expectations and intentions — which is what happened to a manufacturer of dinner plates who had a problem with packaging. The plates were wrapped in old newspapers and packed in boxes. Every packer would eventually slow down to read the papers and look at the pictures. Most employees would drop to about 30 percent efficiency after a few weeks on the job.

The manufacturer tried using other material for packing, but that proved too expensive; the newspapers had been free. They tried using newspapers in different languages, but these were hard to obtain. They even offered incentives to workers to increase the number of plates wrapped, but without great success. Finally, one day in a meeting an exasperated supervisor said they should tape the workers' eyes shut so they couldn't read. This absurd comment created a lot of laughter as the others joked about his comment. But the supervisor had an

"Aha!" moment: he got the idea to hire blind people to do the packing. The company not only greatly increased its packing efficiency but also received tax benefits for hiring the disabled.

Look at the illustration below.

An illustration of squares is your mind's first impression. However, if you focus on the X at the center, circles will appear in the image. The mind, when forced to focus on a subject for a period of time, becomes bored with it and will explore alternative ways of perceiving it by decomposing the whole into parts and then looking for the interesting parts. In this illustration you perceive squares, but your mind soon rearranges them and you perceive a different pattern — circles.

FLAT DADDIES

The same process is apparent in thinking. When you think of an idea, no matter how absurd or silly, your mind will decompose it into parts and then look for the interesting parts to build on. In the early steps of this process, the effects of these changes remain below the level of awareness. After a while, they penetrate consciousness as new ideas and insights. One example of this is an idea developed by the director of the Tri-City Red Cross, an organization that serves the Washington State cities of Kennewick, Pasco, and Richland and supports the families of soldiers deployed in the Middle East.

The director always tried to think up family activities for children of deployed soldiers to keep them connected with their fathers. One day her son suggested that she hire actors to play the part of fathers while they were away. She laughed, but couldn't stop thinking of father substitutes. For a week, she wondered off and on about who or what could double for a deployed soldier. One day she heard about a program based on a children's book, *Flat Stanley*, in which the main character travels the world by envelope. This inspired her brilliant idea.

She had mothers give her pictures of their husbands and the husbands' jacket measurements. Then she made arrangements with a local printer to make life-size pictures of the husbands from the waist up, trim off the background, and back them with foam board. Then she threw a party, where she distributed the pictures to the children, calling them "Flat Daddies" or "Flat Soldiers."

The children were unbelievably overjoyed and began carrying their Flat Daddies with them everywhere. One boy watches football with his Flat Daddy every weekend. Another family eats dinner with their Flat Daddy every night. One mother said she gave her three-year-old daughter a Flat Daddy. At four, her daughter recognized her father when he came home on leave: she yelled, "Daddy, Daddy," when she saw him departing the airplane.

By paying attention to her son's "crazy" idea, the Red Cross director found herself exploring the least likely possibilities both consciously and unconsciously. When you start imagining crazy things, you welcome chance events, such as stumbling across a book about flat Stanley. Logical thinking uses negative emotions to block freedom of thought, and you end up with very few ways to organize information. But when you play around with crazy ideas, you find that your imagination has virtually unlimited ways to organize them.

One technique that will help you discover original ideas is to deliberately provoke unusual thinking patterns by generating a list of directionless, crazy ideas about your subject. This gives you freedom from design and commitment. It will allow you to juxtapose things that would not otherwise be juxtaposed, and to construct a sequence of events which would not otherwise occur.

THOUGHT EXPERIMENT

Imagine you are part of a team of people hired to design a new science building for a college. The college wants a design that has scientific meaning. The challenge is to design something unique that also conveys this meaning.

1. First list as many absurd or fanciful ideas as you can.
   Some examples:
   An invisible building.
   A building whose outside form changes to conform with the weather conditions.
   A building that is animate and whose design changes daily.
   A collapsible building that can be moved around the campus easily.
   A building that talks.
2. Next focus on each idea to extract the principle of the design, the features, and the unique aspects of the idea. List your thoughts and ideas.

Suppose the team members become intrigued with the idea of a building that's alive. They determine the principle to be "life" and decide that some of the attributes of life are as follows:

Breathing: all animals breathe.
Relationships: humans and other animals develop various kinds of relationships.

THOUGHT EXPERIMENT (*CONTINUED*)

Genes: life is genetically determined.
Birth and death: animals are born or hatched, live, and die.
Physical, emotional, and mental states: humans and other animals have physical, emotional, and mental states.

3. Play around with the various aspects of what you perceive as the principles on your list.

In our example, playing with various aspects of life led to the thought of genetics. The team might ask, among other things, "What in building material is analogous to genes?" "Can a building be genetically determined?" "Should we create a brand new species of building?" "Is there a gene pool for buildings?" "Can a building have DNA?"

What's your new building design?

A question that inspired one team of architects was, "Can a building have DNA?" The architects were hired to design a new college building to be named after Agnes Scott. They obtained a sample of Scott's descendant's DNA and had an artist draw a representation of it. Then the artist's rendition of the DNA was inscribed in a four-story-high mural on the outside of the building. It's as if the building visibly represents the invisible Agnes Scott. You can't pass the mural without thinking about her.

What crazy idea can you come up with to promote eggs? A group of food scientists and marketing people were tossing around crazy ideas. One of the suggestions was, "What if eggs talked?" The unique feature was "communication." This led them to develop an egg stamped with a special thermochromic logo that becomes visible when the egg is fully cooked. All you need to decide is whether you want your eggs soft-, medium-, or hard-boiled, and then watch the ink appear. You'll know when the egg is ready by the image that appears.

WALT DISNEY

Using his imagination, Walt Disney uncritically explored fantastical ideas. Afterward, he would engineer these fantasies into feasible ideas and then evaluate them. He would shift his perspective three times by playing three separate and distinct roles in relation to them: those of the dreamer, the realist, and the critic.

On the first day, he would play the dreamer and dream up fantasies and wishful visions. He would let his imagination soar without worrying about how to implement his conceptions. The next day, he would bring his fantasies down to earth by playing the realist. As a realist, he would look for ways to work his conceptions into something practical. On the third day, he would play the part of the critic and poke holes in his ideas, asking, is this feasible?

THOUGHT EXPERIMENT

Challenge: Suppose you own a nightclub and want to issue unique invitations to your grand opening.

Be a dreamer: First, list as many fantastical ideas as you can. Some examples:

Have the invitation magically appear on the invitee's desk.
Have a chair fitted with a sensor so that, when a prospect sits, the chair invites the person.
Guarantee wealth and happiness to all who come.
Create a plant that sprouts an invitation.
Promise that everyone who comes will receive a magic pill that will transform his or her life.

The owners of one nightclub were inspired to make the invitation pill-like. The club sent out a blue pill nestled in a cushion in a black velvet ring box. On the top of the box was written, "This is a magic pill that we guarantee will make you happy." Inside the box the instructions read, "Drop into warm water, stir, and let dissolve." When the pill was immersed, the capsule dissolved and bubbled, and a piece of cellophane with the time, date, and place of the grand opening floated to the top. The invitations cost $1.10 each, and the debut was a smash.

The following table illusion was created by Professor Roger Shepard. Look at the two tables below. They appear to be decidedly different. One is narrow, the other wide. Yet believe it or not, the tables are identical.

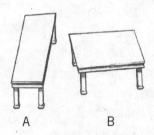

A   B

You can prove this to yourself by cutting out the top of table A, giving it a three-quarter turn to the right, and placing it on the top of table B, or by measuring and comparing the lengths and widths.

Here you take a situation that seems impossible, and, by tinkering, discover that the impossibility is merely an illusion created by the artist's perspective. This points to one of the values of playing with absurd ideas: by tinkering with them, you see things that you normally would miss.

In the following thought experiment are some unusual combinations of objects. This experiment draws on a workshop technique in which participants write random nouns on small slips of paper, which are then randomly combined to suggest unusual objects that participants can contemplate. Combining apparently contradictory or impossible ideas forces participants to stretch and bend their minds to meet the specifications of the task. The objects below are from a past workshop.

THOUGHT EXPERIMENT

Try to imagine each object described in the following list, and draw a picture of it. See if you can imagine each one into something feasible. For example, a piece of furniture that is also a fruit could be designed as a giant pineapple carved into a chair.

A vehicle that is also a kind of fish.
An aquarium that is also a toilet.
A parking meter that is also a kind of person.
A bird that is also a kind of kitchen utensil.
A food flavoring that is also a kind of tool.
A park bench that is also a kind of person.
A computer that is also a kind of teacup.
A cookstove that is also a kind of bicycle.
A lampshade that is also a kind of book.

Some of the ideas this experiment inspired:

- A vehicle that is also a kind of fish: a dolphin-pulled boat.
- A cookstove that is also a kind of bicycle: The tubes of a bicycle frame are filled with steam that can be released to do the cooking. Pedaling functions as the stove's energy source.
- A parking meter that is also a kind of person: The parking meter has infrared sensors and lithium-powered computer chips to "see" parking spaces, much like a person sees. When a car leaves the parking space, the remaining time on the meter is erased.
- An aquarium that is also a toilet: An engineer actually designed a toilet that looks like an aquarium — that is, a toilet with a glass aquarium tank. The toilet's mechanism is hidden behind a wall; a glass aquarium with tiny fishes swimming around appears to take the place of the toilet tank. A restaurant owner bought the toilet as a gimmick, and his business increased as customers told their friends about the toilet.

How about a bench that walks and talks? Visitors to a public square in Cambridge, England, see six benches and six rubbish bins, but this street furniture is very different from what you'd find elsewhere. The benches and bins are equipped with mechanisms and sensors that allow them to move and flock around the square. When no one is sitting on a bench, the bench will move to a new space to make it more attractive for visitors. Often the benches will arrange themselves into different patterns. When it rains, the benches move to protected, drier places. The bins are more solitary and seek quieter spaces to occupy.

The benches and bins drift slowly around the square no faster than a strolling human. Sensors stop them when they get close to other objects. Sometimes, when most of the benches are being sat on, they burst into song, and the bins join in with soprano voices.

IMAGINE

The walking and talking benches and bins are a result of imagination, the power that enables us to visualize and synthesize experiences we have never had. Creative thinkers can imagine themselves in other people's minds, imagine themselves in other people's places, even imagine forces of nature. This is why Einstein often said that imagination is more important than knowledge.

Think of how Einstein changed our understanding of time and space by imagining people going to the center of time in order to freeze their lovers or their children in century-long embraces. This space he imagined is clearly reminiscent of a black hole, where, theoretically, gravity would stop time. Einstein also imagined a woman's heart leaping and falling in love two weeks before she has met the man she loves, which led him to the understanding of acausality, a feature of quantum mechanics. And still another time he imagined a blind beetle crawling around a sphere thinking it was crawling in a straight line.

Try to solve the following thought experiment before you read the paragraph that follows it.

THOUGHT EXPERIMENT

One morning, exactly at sunrise, a Buddhist monk began to climb a tall mountain. The narrow path, no more than a foot or two wide, spiraled around the mountain to a glittering temple at the summit. The monk ascended the path at a varying rate of speed, stopping many times along the way to rest and to eat the dried fruit he carried with him. He reached the temple shortly before sunset. After several days of fasting and meditation, he began his journey back along the same path, starting at sunrise and again walking at a varying speed with many stops along the way. His average speed descending was, of course, greater than his average climbing speed. Is there a spot along the path that the monk will occupy on both trips at precisely the same time of day?

If you try to logically reason this out or use a mathematical approach, you will conclude that it is unlikely for the monk to find himself on the same spot at the same time of day on two different occasions. Instead, visualize the monk walking up the hill, and at the same time imagine the same monk walking down the hill. The two figures must meet at some point in time regardless of their walking speed or how often they stop. Whether the monk descends in two days or three days makes no difference; it all comes out to the same thing.

Now it is, of course, impossible for the monk to duplicate himself and walk up the mountain and down the mountain at the same time. But in the visual image he does; and it is precisely this indifference to logic, this superimposition of one image over the other, that leads to the solution.

The imaginative conception of the monk meeting himself blends the journeys up and down the mountain and superimposes one monk on the other at the meeting place. The ancient Greeks called this kind of thinking *homoios*, which means "same." They sensed that this was really a kind of mirror image of the dream process, and it led to art and scientific revelations.

Imagination gives us the impertinence to imagine making the impossible possible. Einstein, for example, was able to imagine alternatives to the sacred Newtonian notion of absolute time, and discovered that time is relative to your state of motion. Think of the thousands of scientists who must have come close to Einstein's insight but lacked the imagination to see it because of the accepted dogma that time is absolute, and who must have considered it impossible to contemplate any theory.

THOUGHT EXPERIMENT

Think of something in your business that is impossible to do, but that would, if it were possible to do, change the nature of your business forever.

Think of an impossibility, then try to come up with ideas that take you as close as possible to that impossibility. For example, imagine an automobile that is a live, breathing creature. List attributes of living creatures. They are, for example, breathing, growing older, reproducing, feeling emotions, and so on. Then use as many of those attributes as you can while designing your automobile. For instance, can you work emotions into something that a car displays?

Japanese engineers for Toyota are working on a car that they say can express moods ranging from angry to happy to sad. "The car can raise or lower its body height and 'wag' its antenna, and it comes equipped with illuminated hood designs capable of changing colors, which are meant to look like eyebrows, eyes, and even tears. The car will try to approximate the feelings of its driver by drawing on data stored in an onboard computer. So, for example, if another car swerves into an expressive car's lane, the right combination of deceleration, brake pressure, and defensive steering, when matched with previous input from the driver, will trigger an 'angry' look."

The angry look is created as the front end lights up with glowing red U-shaped lights, the headlights become hooded at a forty-five-degree angle, and downward-sloping "eyebrow" lights glow crimson. A good-feeling look is signaled when orange lights illuminate the front end, one headlight winks at the courteous driver, and the car wags its antenna. A sad-feeling look is blue with "tears" dripping from the headlights.

Stretching your imagination by trying to make impossible things possible via concrete thoughts and actions is a mirror reversal of dreaming. Whereas a dream represents abstract ideas as concrete actions and images, this creative process works in the opposite direction, using concrete ideas (a car that is alive) to gain insight on a conscious level and reveal disguised thoughts (about cars showing emotion) as creative imagery.

10 IDEAS FROM GOD

We know more than we can tell.

Imagine a gardener who plants a turnip. After a while, the turnip isn't developing as it should, and the gardener is unhappy. The gardener digs it up and examines the turnip to see if he can find any faults. He then cleans it, clips some roots, and replants the turnip using a different process. By trying to control nature, he has interfered with it and produces a poor turnip, if it grows at all.

The gardener was focused on control and not outcome. When the turnip wasn't developing as it should have, he dug it up and tried another method. If the gardener had relaxed and let nature follow its way, he would have found that nature, with very little help, would do all the work after he planted the seed, and the turnip would grow. All the gardener had to do after he planted the seed was to walk away and do something else.

The same desire to control is what freezes thinking and prevents the free play of awareness and attention. In a way, we are like the gardener who interferes with nature in an attempt to control it.

Look at the following illustration. Focus on the dot and concentrate.

Focusing your attention on the black dot for a period of time makes the shaded background fade and disappear. Imagine the dot is the subject you are thinking about, and the background is the collection of hazy, ambiguous half-formed associations and connections and bits of unrelated thought that are flowing through your mind. Intense focus on your subject makes this treasure trove of information disappear. The more you concentrate, the more these useful associations disappear.

Taking a break and forgetting about the problem allows this information to come back and grow clearer. There is a Chinese term that describes this: *wuwei*, or "not doing." This doesn't mean "doing nothing"; it means "not forcing." Things will open up according to their nature. And they do.

Cognitive scientists have observed that, after a period of incubating their ideas, people are 33 percent more likely to infer connections among distantly related ideas. Yet this enhancement of creative thinking occurs completely beneath the radar — people are more creative after they forget about the problem for a period of time, but they don't know it. It's as if the period of incubation resets your mind. You're taking a walk or taking a shower, and you realize, "Wait a minute, there's another way to do this."

YOU ARE BEING WATCHED

The detective division of a police station had a table with coffee and donuts and a sign that stated, "Help yourself. Please make a contribution of at least one dollar so we can continue offering this service." Few people made a contribution. Most walked away with free coffee and donuts. Psychologists have long been aware of this dismal aspect of human behavior: people are more likely to be honest if they know they're being observed. When nobody's watching, they feel they can get away with murder, or at least with a free cup of coffee.

The secretary who started the practice tried all kinds of ways to encourage contributions, but nothing worked. One day at work she had a tremendous itch on her backside. She carefully looked around to make sure no one was watching, and then scratched the itch, to her great relief. That night while taking a shower, she suddenly got an insight about the coffee station: she could make people feel they were being watched.

Above the coffee and donuts, she taped a poster of a pair of staring eyes. A remarkable thing happened. Soon the contribution jar was overflowing. Apparently, the mere feeling of being watched — even by eyes that were clearly not real — was enough to encourage people to behave honestly. The secretary was stunned. She had expected a small effect, not the response she got. She told the police chief about it. Intrigued, the police chief consulted with psychologists, and they studied the activity and ran a few tests with other kinds of posters. Satisfied that the secret was the "pair of eyes," the chief had posters of eyes slapped all over town as part of a campaign called "We've Got Our Eyes on Criminals." The psychologists are studying the campaign to see if the posters have an effect on things such as car theft and vandalism. The secretary got her insight while not thinking about the problem.

STOP THINKING

A well-known physicist once said that all great discoveries in science were made by scientists not thinking about a specific problem. In the

1970s, Frank Wilczek of the Institute for Advanced Study in Princeton, New Jersey, deduced how the nuclei of atoms stay together, one of those rare "knowing the mind of God" discoveries. His breakthrough occurred when he was reviewing a totally different problem — in fact, a different force of nature. He suddenly experienced a "mind pop" and realized that a failed approach in one area would be successful in another.

Similarly, Bertrand Russell wrote in *The Conquest of Happiness*: "I have found, for example, that, if I have to write upon some rather difficult topic, the best plan is think about it with very great intensity — the greatest intensity of which I am capable — for a few hours or days, and at the end of that time give orders, so to speak, that the work is to proceed underground. After some months I return consciously to the topic and find that the work has been done. Before I had discovered this technique, I used to spend the intervening months worrying because I was making no progress; I arrived at the solution none the sooner for this worry, and the intervening months were wasted."

Incubation usually involves setting a problem aside for a few hours, days, or weeks and moving on to other projects. This allows the subconscious to continue to work on the original challenge. The more interested you are in solving the challenge, the more likely your subconscious will generate ideas. The creative act owes little to logic or reason. In their accounts of the circumstances under which big ideas occurred to them, scientists have often mentioned that the inspiration had no relation to the work they happened to be doing. Sometimes it came while they were traveling, shaving, or thinking about other matters. It seems that the creative process cannot be summoned at will or even on demand. It seems to occur when the mind is relaxed and the imagination is roaming.

Illusory gray spots mysteriously appear at the points of intersection in the following black and white grid. However, a gray spot does not occur at the specific intersection on which you concentrate your attention.

Sometimes ideas, like the gray spots, do not appear when you are concentrating, and they mysteriously appear when you are not. Modern science recognizes this phenomenon of incubation and insight and yet cannot account for it. This suggests how the creative act came to be associated with divine inspiration, for the illumination appears to be involuntary.

The composer Paul Hindemith described it this way: "We all know what it's like to see a heavy flash of lightning in the night. Within a second's time we see a broad landscape, not only in its general outline, but also every detail." Although we could never describe every single component of the picture, we feel that not even the smallest leaf of grass escapes our attention. "We experience a view that is comprehensive and, at the same time, immensely detailed," one we could never have under normal daylight conditions. Our nerves and senses may feel strained by the suddenness of the event. The French genius Henri Poincaré spoke of incredible ideas and insights that came to him with the suddenness and certainty of a heavy flash of lightning in the night. The sudden arrival of an idea may seem so dramatic that the precise moment can be remembered in unusual detail.

CLOUDS OF THOUGHT

Think of thoughts as atoms hanging by hooks on the sides of your mind. When you think about a subject, some of these thoughts become loose and begin to move around in your subconscious mind. The more work you put into thinking about a problem, the more thoughts and bits of information you set in random motion. Your subconscious mind never rests. When you quit thinking about the subject and decide to forget it, your subconscious mind doesn't quit working. Your thoughts keep colliding, combining, and making associations.

In mathematics, the factorial calculates how many ways you can combine things. If you have three objects, then there are one times two times three, which leaves six combinations. Mathematicians calculate that ten bits of information can combine and recombine in three million different ways in your mind. So you can imagine the cloud of thoughts combining and making associations when you incubate problems.

Try the following thought experiment.

THOUGHT EXPERIMENT

Have someone slowly read this list out loud. (If you don't have anyone handy, read the list to yourself, then close the book.) Take three minutes to write down all the words you remember.

sour nice candy
honey sugar soda
bitter pie good
heart taste cake
tooth tart chocolate

Compare the words you wrote down to the original list.

Most people falsely remember the word *sweet* as being on the list. The word isn't there, but it is related to the words that are on the list. Thinking is associative, and thinking about one thing can get you thinking about related things.

I came across an interesting parallel for this process while reading a comment by Rupert Sheldrake about plant physiology: "Annual plants, which die after fruiting, have no need to keep anything in reserve. They give all they have got, continuing to form fruits until they run out of resources, with the result that the later-formed fruits get smaller and smaller. By contrast, in perennial plants, which need to keep something in reserve for the next year, the fruits formed early and late in the season are more or less the same size. Perennial plants yield less than their full capacity, because they hold back reserves for the following season." We are like perennials, in a way: when we are working on a problem, we reach a point when our brains shut down. Perhaps this is nature's way of helping us hold something in reserve for future thought, after the information has been incubated for a period of time.

Following is a procedure that is remarkably effective in tapping the subconscious.

THOUGHT EXPERIMENT

Work on a problem until you have mulled over all the relevant pieces of information. Talk with others about the problem, ask questions, and do as much research as you can until you are satisfied that you have pushed your conscious mind to its limit.

Write a letter to your unconscious mind about the problem. Make the letter as detailed and specific as possible. Define the problem, describe its attributes, what steps you have taken, the difficulties, the gaps, what is needed, what you want, and so on. Just writing the letter will help better define the problem, clarify issues, point out where more informa-tion is needed, and prepare your unconscious to work on a solution. The letter should read as if it were written to a real person. Imagine that your unconscious is all-knowing and can solve any problem that is properly stated.

THOUGHT EXPERIMENT (*CONTINUED*)

Instruct your unconscious to find the solution. Write, "Your mission is to find the solution to the problem. I would like the solution in two days." Seal the letter and put it away. You may even want to mail it to yourself.

Let go of the problem. Don't work on it. Forget it. Do something else. This is the incubation stage, when much of what goes on occurs outside your focused awareness, in your unconscious. Open the letter in two days. If the problem still has not been solved, write on the bottom of the letter, "Let me know the minute you solve this," and put it away. Sooner or later, when you are most relaxed and removed from the problem, the answer will magically pop into your mind.

Bert, the creative director of an advertising agency, told me about a letter he addressed to his subconscious mind, which he called "Secret Expert":

How are you, Secret Expert?

I haven't heard from you in some time, so I thought I would write you a letter. I need your help with a problem. I need to come up with an exciting new marketing program to introduce a new season of television shows. The shows include programs about criminal forensics, contests for prizes, lawyer shows, and comedies. I'm interested in coming up with some kind of campaign that will capture the audience's attention more than one time. The approach of the campaign should be unique and unexpected.

We've had several meetings but keep coming up with the same old traditional marketing campaign ideas. What do people need and keep? Is there something they need that we can advertise on? What kind of goods, products, foods, and services should we investigate? What producers, distributors, and retailers should we study? Can we combine our services with another company? Do we need to share revenue? I need a fresh approach to advertising. Your mission is to give me a new idea on how to advertise television shows. I need the idea in two days. Help!!!

Thanks,
Bert

Bert mailed the letter to himself, and two days later received it. When he read what he had written, he got his brainstorm, which was to advertise on eggs. Where did the connection come from? Was it an association between "foods," "need," "producers," and "fresh approach," as in "fresh eggs?"

He arranged to place laser imprints of the network's logo, as well as the names of some of its shows, on eggs — 35 million of them. Here are some of the shows and their planned slogans, as reported in the *New York Times*: *CSI* ("Crack the case on CBS"), *The Amazing Race* ("Scramble to win on CBS"), and *Shark* ("Hard-boiled drama"). The ads for the network's Monday night lineup of comedy shows included "Shelling out laughs," "Funny side up," and "Leave the yolks to us."

As the article noted, most shoppers will look at eggs more than once. They look at them in the store to see if they are not damaged, when they take them out of carton and place them in the refrigerator, and when they are ready to use them and crack them open. Eggs are unlike any other ad medium in the world, because you look at this medium while using the product. Once egg producers, distributors, and retailers discovered they would all share in the ad revenue, they all loved the concept.

Here is another thought experiment to try the next time you're seeking to ignite your subconscious mind.

THOUGHT EXPERIMENT

1. First draw three abstract compositions using forms of any type or shape. Work fast; use your intuition.
2. Select one. Identify features of that selection that contribute most to its essential character. For example, an abstract shape might suggest the form of something smooth and fast, slow and chunky, thick, sketchy, or wiry, and so on.
3. Draw another picture, one that captures the essential gesture of the lines and shapes of your first drawing. Do not reproduce it exactly. The idea is to capture its essence.
4. Study the drawing and imagine what it represents. What could it represent? A cloud, the ocean, a cat, a baby's face, a soldier, a car, and so on.
5. Finally, conceptually blend what you see in the drawing with your challenge.

A designer imagined his final drawing represented a buzzing bee. This got him thinking about the relationship between design and nature. He thought about bees and the products they create, such as beeswax and beehives. He decided to make vases from beeswax. He discovered by accident that, when placed in beeswax vases — which contain propolis, an antibacterial agent that protects against biological decay — flowers lasted longer than in glass ones.

We all have the feeling that we know more than we can tell. If I put a picture of your best friend's face among a million other faces, you'll be able to pick it out. Yet you will not be able to verbalize how you did that.

Walt Whitman wrote in *Leaves of Grass*, "I believe a leaf of grass is no less than the journey-work of the stars." How did he come up with that? How could he know that the entire universe shares a common set of elements? Was he born knowing what supernova nucleosynthesis is? Where did he learn that the elements were created far away in space, in the explosions of stars? How could he know that stars eject most of their mass during supernovas, giving birth to the elements, which, on Earth, then assembled themselves into everything, even a leaf of grass? Did he have some deep memory of coming from the stars? Is this why we find his poetry comprehensible and beautiful?

The following experiment is remarkably successful in flushing out obscure thoughts, hunches, and combinations from your subconscious. It's also a favorite writer's exercise for overcoming writer's block.

THOUGHT EXPERIMENT

Set aside ten minutes. Simply list whatever comes to mind (words, phrases, thought fragments, etc.). What you are doing is trying to catch thoughts and feelings from your subconsciousness. When you are finished, don't review what you have written. It's important to do this ten-minute exercise every day for five days without reviewing your list.

On day six go back over each day's writing, starting with day one. Circle the phrases, thoughts, and metaphors that hold the greatest interest for you. List the items you've circled. Then look for patterns, relationships, and insights into things you have been working on.

You'll discover glimpses of relationships between thoughts, facts, or experiences that were kept separate from each other in your conscious mind. Your subconscious mind brings out intuitive connections.

Jack is a schoolteacher who had been leading discussions with concerned students about the environment and sustainability. For five days, he listed whatever came to his mind, then he reviewed his list, looking for thought fragments and patterns. Some of his circled thoughts were "poor in Africa," "soap and water," "cleanliness is next to godliness," "Red Cross," "ways to recycle water in hotels," and so on.

Reviewing his thoughts, he combined "soap," "recycling," and "hotels" into an idea. He thought of all those little bars of soap you get in hotels. People use them once or twice, and then they are discarded. He created a volunteer organization to collect all the leftover soap from about two hundred hotels and bed-and-breakfast establishments in his city. The hotels get a tax break for donating the used soap to a charitable cause. His group sanitizes the soap and recycles it by donating it to homeless shelters in the United States and in El Salvador, Honduras, and Nicaragua, where soap is needed.

WHAT DO AN EGG AND YOUR SUBCONSCIOUS HAVE IN COMMON?

Imagine an egg sitting in its nest of straw, Silvia Hartmann writes.

> It doesn't do anything and makes no sound. It doesn't change shape, it doesn't change color. It doesn't pulsate. It doesn't roll around. You could look at it for days and days and you'd come away thinking that it was an inert object, that there was nothing going on in it.
>
> Yet inside the egg a riot of change is taking place — a storm of reorganization, feeding, and growth — as a bunch of random cells become an entity. This growing entity becomes ever more defined and more complex, more organized in every way, more mature, more fantastic, with every heartbeat.
>
> One day the egg that lay motionless for so long and seemed to be inert will begin to rock, and then it will crack, and then a bird will emerge, eventually spread its wings for the first time, and take its first small steps.

I think of the egg as a beautiful metaphor for your subconscious mind. The subconscious mind is a wonderful resource. Once you learn how to listen to it, it's like listening to an egg cracking open, followed by more and more unconventional thoughts that emerge from your subconscious like tiny birds emerging from their eggs.

PART 2

The Creative Thinker

Don't be the person who sees the sun as a yellow spot in the sky; be the person who sees a yellow spot on a grimy sidewalk as the sun.

In our society today, there is an almost universal tendency to ignore the dynamic interconnectedness of all things. When you look at the illustration of two concentric circles and focus on the dot, and then move your head slowly toward and away from the illustration, a remarkable thing happens. The circles in this two-dimensional diagram begin to rotate. This is supposedly not possible, and yet you see it. For this illusion to work, you need the slanted shapes that make up the circles to be properly arranged, the dot to focus on, and your own interaction with the illustration as you move your head forward and back. Change any of these parts or the way they interact (for example, don't move your head), and then the illustration becomes lifeless.

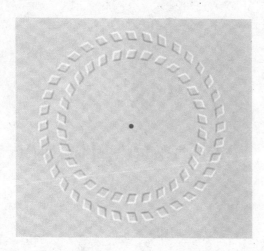

Similarly, there are a number of parts that make up a creative-thinking person, all of which are interconnected. If you change one part you affect all parts.

To continue further, think of the sentence "The mouse is confined in a box." A box can be made by nailing six boards together. But it's obvious that no box can hold a mouse unless the box has "containment." If you study each board, you will discover that no single board has any containment, since the mouse can just walk away from it. And if there is no containment in one board, there can't be any in six boards. So the box can have no containment at all. Theoretically, then, the mouse should be able to escape.

What keeps the mouse confined? Of course it is the way a box prevents motion in all directions, because each board bars escape in a certain direction. The left side keeps the mouse from going left; the right keeps it from going right; the top keeps it from leaping out; and so on. The secret of a box lies in how the boards are arranged to prevent motion in all directions! That's what *containing* means. So it's silly to expect any separate board by itself to effect containment.

The reason a box does not seem mysterious is that we understand perfectly that no single board can contain by itself, and that the boards of a well-made box interact to prevent motion in any direction. Something similar applies to the word *creative*. It is foolish to use this word to describe the smallest components of a process, because this word was invented to describe how larger assemblies interact. Like *containment*, the word *creative* is used for describing phenomena that result from certain combinations of relationships.

Similarly, the creative thinker is a result of the assembly and interactions of certain critical human traits. First, you must have the intention and desire to be creative; second, you must consciously cultivate positive speaking and thinking patterns; and last, you must act like a creative thinker and go through the motions of being creative every day. These are the subjects of the next three chapters.

INTENTION IS THE SEED OF CREATIVE THINKING

*It is not because things are
difficult that we do not dare;
it is because we do not dare
that they are difficult.*

—— SENECA

Many of us have the illusion that we think comprehensively, but we don't. We cannot take in massive amounts of information, assimilate it, and make it valuable in any meaningful way; we take in information in sequence. It isn't possible to simultaneously process multiple potent stimuli and do it effectively. You can demonstrate this to yourself by performing the following thought experiment.

THOUGHT EXPERIMENT

Visualize the alphabet in capital letters.

A...Z

How many letters have "curved" lines in them?

Notice how you think. You see the letters flash before you one by one, sequentially, not spontaneously. It's like watching a slide show. We think no faster than the speed of life. If you are still uncertain, try counting forward to one hundred by threes, and backward by seven simultaneously.

Because we think sequentially and no faster than the speed of life, we cannot pay attention to everything effectively. Our attention becomes too scattered to be of any use. You'll find that your intention will create criteria, which will determine what — out of the range of possible experiences — you are attending to at the time, and this will help you reach your goal.

Let us imagine that your intention is to make a canoe. You will have, at first, some idea of the kind of canoe you wish to make. You will visualize the canoe, then you will go into the woods and look at the trees. Your desired outcome will determine your criteria for the tree you need. Your criteria might involve the size, usefulness, and beauty of the tree, and your design. Criteria both filter your perceptions and invest a particular situation with meaning, informing your experience and behavior at the time. Out of the many trees in the woods, you will end up focusing on the few that meet your criteria, until you find the perfect tree.

You will cut the tree down; remove the branches from the trunk; take off the bark; hollow out the trunk; carve the outside shape of the hull; form the prow and the stern; and then perhaps carve decorations on the prow. In this way you will produce the canoe.

The process is so ordinary, so simple, so direct that we fail to see the beauty and simplicity of it. You have the intention to make a canoe, visualize an outcome, and give birth to something whole, a canoe. Your intention to make a canoe gives you direction and also imposes criteria on your choices, consciously and unconsciously.

Intention has a way of bringing to our awareness only those things that our brains deem important. You'll begin to see ideas for your canoe pop up everywhere in your environment. You'll see them in tables, in magazines, on television, and in other structures while walking down the street. You'll see them in the most unlikely things — such as a refrigerator — that you use every day without giving them much thought. How the brain accomplishes such miracles is one of neuroscience's great mysteries.

THOUGHTS ARE TINY SPINS

We all played with magnets when we were children. A magnetized object consists of a multitude of tiny little elements called "spins" (see the illustration). Each spin has a particular orientation corresponding to the direction of its magnetic field. In general, these spins point in different directions, so that their magnetic fields cancel each other out (disordered spins are illustrated on the left). Spins pointing in opposite directions repel each other, like the north poles of two magnets that are brought together.

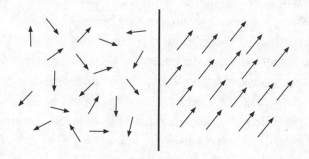

However, when the temperature decreases, the spins spontaneously align themselves so that they all point the same direction. Instead of canceling each other, the different magnetic fields now support each other, producing a strong overall pattern. Spins pointing in the same direction attract each other, like the north pole of one magnet attracting the south pole of another magnet. Magnetization is a good example of how forces aligned in the same direction attract and reinforce each other to create a dynamic, natural pattern. In the image on the left, the pattern is inconsistent and incoherent, while in the image on the right, the pattern is straight, coherent, and dynamic.

Think of your thoughts as tiny spins in your brain. If you have no intention to be or to do something, your thoughts are disordered, with no direction, much like the tiny spins on the left. When you have a real intention to be or to do something, your thoughts have purpose and automatically align with each other to form a dynamic mental state of awareness aimed in the direction of the intention.

This mental state is evident in the work of Hashem Akbari, an environmentalist activist and a scientist at the Lawrence Berkeley National Laboratory, who is always thinking of ways to offset carbon dioxide emissions. His intention to help save the environment guides his observations in daily life. One day he noticed a house with a white roof that reminded him of the "large white structures in the Iranian desert that he saw as a child. The structures captured the night wind to cool the buildings, keeping the people inside comfortable."

This observation startled him because he realized that dark materials absorb heat, and that if roofs were white they would reflect heat. Musing, he wondered what the effect would be if all roofs were white. After making a study of the matter, he concluded that, if the hundred largest cities in the world replaced their dark roofs with white surfaces, and their asphalt-based roads with concrete or other light-colored materials, it could offset 44 billion tons of carbon dioxide. According to Akbari's Island Group, "this is equivalent to taking the world's approximately 600 million cars off the road for 18 years."

Akbari's intention tuned his brain to a higher level, which substantially increased the likelihood of his noticing opportunities in his environment. As Scott Adams writes, "Your brain processes only a tiny portion of your environment at a time. It risks being overwhelmed by the volume of information that bombards you every waking moment. Your brain compensates by filtering out the 99.9 percent of your environment that doesn't matter to you."

THOUGHT EXPERIMENT

If you came across this list of five items, it would be meaningless. You would ignore it and move on. However, if I tell you that all five have parts in common with parts of a human face, and challenge you to think of what these parts are, you will — that is, if you have the intention to do so. Intention will tune your mind to a higher level, increasing the likelihood of your finding the answers.

Cannons
Footballs
Gears
Potatoes
Shoes
(Answers at end of chapter.)

Intention works. Try another simple experiment: Focus on a penny. Visualize it. Now say to yourself silently that you are going to find a penny on the ground. Then, look for the penny every time you take a walk. Concentrate on finding a penny. After you find a penny, go looking for a second one. How long did it take to find the first penny? Compare the time it takes to find the second penny with the time it took to find the first. Now look for a third, fourth, fifth, and so on. You will amaze yourself with the number of lost pennies on the ground that you previously did not see.

Now look at the illustration with blobs (see next page). Before you read further, think for a moment and imagine what it could represent. No doubt you can imagine a variety of things. The blobs could represent a map of part of the world, a child's face, a view of the earth from a satellite, white paint splattered on a black wall, a view of the sky through jungle foliage, an alien life-form, energy forces caused by oppositional political views, hidden faces — in fact, anything at all.

Now suppose I tell you there is a cow hidden in the illustration, and I ask you to find it. If you take the attitude that there cannot be a cow in the illustration or that, perhaps, there may or may not be a cow in the drawing, it will be difficult to find the cow. You'll spend your time and energy imagining all the reasons why there is no cow. But if you believe there is a cow and intend to find the cow, you will find it. Think, "I must find the cow." It may take minutes, but it will emerge. You will see the face of a cow staring back at you.

How is this possible? How can you see a cow simply by looking for a cow in a sketch of meaningless blobs? The drawing does not change. Your eyes do not change or improve. The only change is your intention. Your intention to find a cow generates your mental awareness of the cow. This awareness organizes the blobs in various ways in your mind until you see a cow.

GOING THROUGH THE MOTIONS

THOUGHT EXPERIMENT

Take out a sheet of paper and at least ten items — money, credit cards, keys, coins, and so on. Create an assemblage by using the following guidelines: Imagine an assemblage that metaphorically represents you.

THOUGHT EXPERIMENT (*CONTINUED*)

Do not think about the materials you have in hand. Instead think about the shape you would like your assemblage to have. What are the rhythms you want? The texture? Where do you want it to be active? Passive? Where do things overlap, and where are they isolated? Think in general and of the overall picture, and leave out the details. Do not think about trying to create great art; just think about who you are and how you can represent yourself metaphorically.

Now form a more specific idea of the final assemblage. As you look at the paper, imagine the detailed assemblage you want to create. Make sure you've formed this image before you move on to the next step.

Place the items on the paper. Since the composing stage is already done, it's time to bring your creation into physical existence.

When you're done, decide how closely the finished composition comes to your conception. Critique your assemblage. Look at it for its own sake, independent of the fact that you have created it. Then take the items off the paper and repeat the same procedure. Make the assemblage again.

By conceptualizing and using materials you had on hand, you created an artistic assemblage from nothing. If you performed this exercise every day with different objects, you would become an artist who specializes in rearranging different objects into art. Your intention, and the activity of creating, spark synaptic transmissions in your brain, and these turn on the genes linked to what you are doing — you are responding to an environmental challenge (making an assemblage).

I like to compare this to weight lifting. If you want to build muscles, you lift weights. Those genes are turned on only in response to an environmental challenge. That's why you've got to keep lifting heavier and heavier weights — the phrase "No pain, no gain" may be literally true in this case. Interaction with the environment turns on certain genes that otherwise wouldn't be turned on; in fact, they will be turned off if certain challenges aren't being faced.

The same is true of thought processes. When you are thinking unconventionally and producing creative ideas, you are replenishing neurotransmitters linked to genes that are being turned on and off in response to what the brain is doing, which in turn is responding to challenges. When you go through the motions of creating an assemblage, you are energizing your brain by increasing the number of contacts between neurons. The more times you act, the more active your brain becomes and the more creative you become.

INTENTION BOARD

Experimental social psychologists have conducted numerous experiments that demonstrate how behavior and performance can be "primed" by showing participants certain objects and pictures. In one study, participants who were primed with pictures associated with business — such as briefcases, pens, pictures of people dressed in business clothes, commuter trains, and so on — became more competitive. The social psychologist Michael Slepian and colleagues at Tufts University noticed during a study on "bright ideas" that participants became more insightful and creative when they were primed with an exposed lightbulb. In short, they found that even exposure to an illuminating lightbulb primes creativity.

One way to prime yourself for creativity is to generate an awareness of what you want to be or accomplish. You can do this by creating an "intention board." An intention board is a large poster board on which you paste images, sayings, articles, poems, and other items that you've collected from magazines and other sources. It's simple. The idea is to surround yourself with images of your intention (what you want to create or who you want to become) and, in the process, to encourage your awareness and passion to grow. Lay your intention board on a surface where you can work on it, and try out this thought experiment.

THOUGHT EXPERIMENT

Ask yourself what it is you want to be or to create. Maybe one word will be the answer. Maybe images will appear in your head. Post the word or image in the middle of your intention board.

Suppose you want to create a new business. Post the words "New Business" or a picture that represents a new business in the center of the board. Now look through magazines and other sources and pull out pictures, poems, articles, or headlines that relate to entrepreneurs and new business ventures. Have fun with it. Make a big pile of images, words, and phrases. Go through the pile and put favorites on the board. If you add new ones, eliminate those that no longer feel right. This is where intuition comes in. As you place the items on the board, you'll get a sense how they should be laid out. For instance, you might want to assign a theme to each corner of the board, such as "What I have," "What I will have," "What I need," and "How to get what I need."

Hang the board on a wall and keep adding new pieces that you feel have more relevance and removing those that no longer work. Study and work on it every day. You'll discover that the board will add clarity to your desires, and feeling to your visions, which in turn will generate an awareness of the things in your environment that can help you realize your vision.

My brother-in-law desired to be an artist. His intention board was a collage of pictures of paintings and artists, poetry about art, and articles about artists and their work. Over time, he began to imagine conversing with his various prints of paintings. One print that particularly enthralled him was Vincent van Gogh's *Starry Night*. He would focus on the painting and engage in an imaginary two-way conversation. The more he engaged with the painting, the more alive it seemed to become. He would ask the painting questions, such as, What inspired the artist to paint the picture? What was his knowledge of the world? What were his contemporaries' views of the painting? How was the artist able to communicate over the centuries? What is the artist communicating? He would ask how the colors worked together, and ask questions about lines, shapes, and styles.

My brother-in-law, once a disgruntled government employee, is now a successful artist who has had several showings of his work, at which he sold pieces. He created an environment with his intention board that influenced his insight into art and his role in the world. The board primed his subconscious mind, which influenced his psychology.

Imagine a person who is aware of all the colors "except one particular shade of blue. Let all the different shades of blue, other than that one, be placed before him, arranged in order from the deepest to the lightest shade of blue. He most probably will perceive a blank, where that one shade is missing," and will realize that the distance is greater between the contiguous colors than between any others. He will then imagine what this particular shade should look like, though he has never seen it. This would not be possible had he not seen all the different shades of blue.

Similarly, as your board evolves and becomes more and more sophisticated, you will perceive blanks where something is missing. You will then begin to imagine ways to fill in the blanks in order to realize your vision.

See if you can solve the following experiment before you read further.

THOUGHT EXPERIMENT

Here is the 8 of diamonds. Can you find another 8 among these diamonds?

Your brain becomes an extraordinary pattern-recognition tool when you focus your intention. In addition to identifying what's missing, you will begin to think of alternatives that can substitute for what is "missing" from your intention board. You will find yourself seeing more than what's there. In the preceding experiment, the additional 8 can be found in the negative (white) space between the diamonds.

An inventor I know uses one whole wall in his workshop to post articles, pictures, photos, personal notes, and so on. He ruminates by his wall almost daily. His general theme is "supply and demand." He is constantly identifying demands and then trying to invent something to supply them at a profit. His wall has pictures of people scalping football tickets, people trying to make reservations for seats at premier restaurants or for Broadway shows, traffic jams in New York that develop as people look for parking spaces, a clock showing the passing of time, and many other things.

One day he posted a short article about a municipality on the verge of bankruptcy. That got him thinking about what a municipality might supply to meet a demand. He observed his pictures of cars, parking lots, traffic jams, and clocks, and one photo of parking meters on an empty street. He thought that one thing a municipality has to sell is time — most cities do sell time by renting out space in parking lots and alongside parking meters.

Parking meters inspired his idea. Parking meters provide income, but he wondered if they could be better designed to correlate with actual demand. He designed a parking system that adjusts the price of parking spaces according to demand at any given moment. The system uses electronic sensors to measure the call for parking slots in real time, and prices them accordingly. So when there are a lot of empty parking spaces, you can pay as little as twenty-five cents an hour. When space is at a premium, you will have to shell out up to six dollars an hour.

INTENTION INFLUENCES EVEN
PHYSIOLOGICAL FUNCTIONS

A remarkable experiment at Columbia University demonstrated that women who sought services in a fertility clinic were almost twice as likely to get pregnant when they prayed to get pregnant. What is prayer but an expression of intention and desire? Women who prayed had a pregnancy rate of about 50 percent, versus 26 percent for women who did not pray.

When the women prayed, their mental state changed from "I would like to" to "I will" get pregnant. Yes, intention influences even your physiological functions. Here's a simple experiment you can do anywhere that demonstrates this.

THOUGHT EXPERIMENT

Place two objects in front of you, within your reach but at different distances. Your goal is to touch them simultaneously when given a "go" signal. It is well known that the movement time for a single limb depends on the distance the limb has to move and the precision requirements of the target. What happens when the two hands must move in different directions to targets at different distances?

First, make a conscious intention to reach them simultaneously. Think, "I must reach them at the same time." Next, say "go" and reach for the targets. You'll discover that both limbs reach both targets practically simultaneously. In other words, your intention influences your brain to coordinate both limbs as a single functional unit.

WHY THE GEESE DID NOT FLY

Many people love to think of and talk about something they would like to do, create, or discover. They read books about it, go to lectures and seminars, discuss it with friends, admire people who actually do it, and may even write about it. It is the thinking and talking that fascinates them, not the actual doing. The philosopher Søren Kierkegaard expressed this thought best in a parable, which has been paraphrased in an anonymous English translation quoted by Athol Gill in *The Fringes of Freedom.*

A certain flock of geese lived together in a barnyard with high walls around it. Because the corn was good and the barnyard was secure, these geese would never take a risk. One day a philosopher goose came among them. He was a very good philosopher, and every week they listened quietly and attentively to his learned discourses. "My fellow travelers on the way of life," he would say, "can you seriously imagine that this barnyard, with great, high walls around it, is all there is to existence?

"I tell you, there is another and a greater world outside, a world of which we are only dimly aware. Our forefathers knew of this outside world. For did they not stretch their wings and fly across the trackless wastes of desert and ocean, of green valley and wooded hill? But alas, here we remain in this barnyard, our wings folded and tucked into our sides, as we are content to puddle in the mud, never lifting our eyes to the heavens, which should be our home."

The geese thought this was very fine lecturing. "How poetical," they thought. "How profoundly existential. What a flawless summary of the mystery of existence." Often the philosopher spoke of the advantages of flight, calling on the geese to be what they were. After all, they had wings, he pointed out. What were wings for, but to fly with? Often he reflected on the beauty and the wonder of life outside the barnyard, and the freedom of the skies. And every week the geese were uplifted, inspired, moved by the philosopher's message. They hung on his every word. They devoted hours, weeks, months to a thoroughgoing analysis and critical evaluation of his doctrines. They produced learned treatises on the ethical and spiritual implications of flight. All this they did. But one thing they never did. They did not fly! For the corn was good, and the barnyard was secure.

ANSWER KEY:
Cannons have mouths.
Footballs have noses.
Gears have teeth.
Potatoes have eyes.
Shoes have tongues.

CHANGE THE WAY YOU SPEAK, AND YOU CHANGE THE WAY YOU THINK

*Why do we speak in deficit by describing
what is missing, what is excluded,
what's wrong, what's not there?*

We often describe things, good or bad, in terms of what they are not. For example, this morning I ran into an old friend and asked him how he was feeling. He answered, "No complaints." Now, what does that mean? Does it mean he has a list of complaints taped on his bedroom wall that he reads every morning to see if he has anything to complain about?

Pay attention to how your friends and colleagues talk. You will find that many speak a language of exclusion, a language about "what is not," instead of "what is" or "what can be." You give an idea to your supervisor at work and you hear, "Not bad." Does that mean every other idea you offered was bad? You suggest that you implement a new plan or idea and you hear, "It won't hurt." Does that mean that everything else you implemented did hurt?

How many times have you heard a friend say

to you something like, "Why don't we get together for lunch?" What's interesting is that when someone asks another person "Why don't we," the receiver frequently replies with some type of "no." When someone says, "Why don't we...?" our first unconscious impulse may be to begin to think of reasons why not to get together. The phrasing creates ambivalence. However, if you were to change the question to "How about getting together on Monday?" or "Let's get together on Monday," the ambivalence would disappear.

THINK "YES"

Because most adults focus on deficiencies, they phrase some of their thoughts and ideas with negatives such as *no, never, don't,* and *not.* As you read this, you might be thinking, "I never would have thought of that" or "Not a bad insight." Rephrase your thought to "This is the first time I ever thought about that." Or "That's an exciting insight that could explain a lot." Notice how the switch from "what is not" to "what is" affects your perception of the information. You now feel interest, curiosity, surprise, and even fascination. You can feel your consciousness expand.

Children, before they become educated, speak a different language, a language of inclusion, a language of "what is" and "what can be." If you ask children how they feel, they'll tell you. They'll say, "Great," or "Awesome," or "Sleepy," or "I'm sick." Offer an idea to a child, and the child will reply, "Great" or "Interesting."

Suppose you go to Disneyland with your family, and you have a wonderful time. I come up to you and ask, "How did you like Disneyland?" If your response is "Not bad," that description of what is not may come across in a cool monotone barren of enthusiasm.

But what if you say, "Great"? Notice that there is a difference in volume, in affect, in intonation — in the whole feeling associated with the word *great.* Your volume goes up. Your mouth gets more relaxed. Your thoughts and feelings are different when you talk about what's there, as opposed to what's missing.

By changing your language and speaking patterns in a positive way, so that they are about "what's there," you guarantee a feeling of optimism and real output in performance. What you say affects how you feel. How you feel affects how you think, and vice versa. All language, feelings, and thoughts interact with each other, and the entire accumulation of those influences creates your output and behavior. This is illustrated in a behavior triangle.

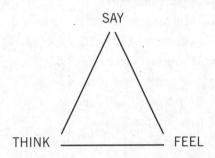

Thought is not different from emotion. Suppose a friend keeps you waiting for two hours. You can get angry, thinking, "What does he mean, treating me like this? He has no concern, no consideration for me. He's always treating me badly," and so on. By thinking in this way, you get very angry. Then, when he arrives and explains that he was late because of an accident that held up traffic, the anger dissipates. This shows that the emotion was influenced by thought. If you change your thought, the anger fades.

CHANGE THE WAY YOU SPEAK, AND YOU CHANGE THE WAY YOU FEEL

If you change one element — your language — your thoughts and feelings will be changed as well. The cumulative impact will be new patterns of output and behavior. The language corner of the triangle is easier to control than the other two. This is where you can make a conscious decision to become a positive-thinking person by creating positive speaking patterns.

Once I stayed at the storied Ritz-Carlton in Montreal. Usually I don't like staying in expensive hotels. Yet in the Ritz I felt great. I discussed my feelings with the manager, and he told me his secret. He told me that the most significant factor for their success was training their employees to frame everything they say in a positive manner. For example, employees who perform services for you will say, "It's a pleasure," instead of something like "No problem," when you thank them. Or "Our restaurant would be pleased to serve you tonight," instead of "Why don't you visit our restaurant?" Guests feel welcome and appreciated, and find themselves feeling happy and positive. By the end of my stay, I was framing everything I had to say in a positive way. The Ritz-Carlton experience demonstrates how language allows us to influence ourselves and others in a particular way — we can transfer our own mental state to another's mind.

Lera Boroditsky, a professor of psychology, neuroscience, and symbolic systems at Stanford University, has written about the ways in which our language shapes the way we think about such basic subjects as space, time, and color. You can discover this phenomenon for yourself by performing the following thought experiment with a small group.

THOUGHT EXPERIMENT

Pass out pendulums to several people and divide the participants into two groups. Tell one group to hold the pendulum steady, and tell the other group to hold it steady but also not to move the pendulum sideways.

Participants in the latter group will invariably move the pendulums sideways, while the group you tell to simply hold them steady will not. Why? Because thinking about not having to move an object sideways activates the very muscles that move it that way. The words you use to instruct the participants alter their perceptual and connotative thinking processes.

Starting any behavior pattern is easier than stopping one. It's easier to concentrate on starting to breathe clean air, starting to eat more healthy foods, starting to learn to relax, starting to hit the golf ball down the fairway, and starting to be more upbeat by changing your speaking patterns. Stripping negatives from your speech pattern and speaking about "what is," instead of "what is not," will, over time, cultivate a positive attitude and change your perspective on your work and, indeed, on life itself.

THOUGHT EXPERIMENT

My mother is a positive, happy person and was the first to teach me that word choice determines thought choice, and that the latter determines emotions and actions. She constantly corrected my speech whenever I complained or was otherwise negative, and when I said something bad about another person. I tried hard to correct my speech, but I found it is not enough to try to stop being negative. It requires conditioning.

My mother designed a solution in the form of a simple green rubber band, which she asked me to wear while accepting this challenge: I was to go twenty days without complaining or being negative. Each time I complained, I had to switch the rubber band to the other wrist and start again from day zero. It was an incredibly simple way for me to understand my own thoughts and the factors that influence my thinking. The effects of this little exercise were immediate and life changing.

Fix the words and you fix your thoughts. Try this as an experiment for twenty days, and I bet you'll find it as effective as I did.

It has become evident, through the work of linguists, anthropologists, and psychologists, that language and thought cannot be separated. Language is not an arbitrary set of symbols. Instead, it is a manifestation of perceptual and connotative processes. But it is more than that. Words and syntax not only reveal — they influence as well. You can use words to express good or to express evil, as pictured in the illustration.

For example, a politician who opposes allowing homosexuals in the military would phrase a question this way: "Should we not allow gays into the military?" Conversely, if the politician reframed his question as "Should we allow gays into the military?" his prejudice would be psychologically reduced by the choice of words.

WORDS PRIME THE WAY YOU THINK

As I've already mentioned, language influences behavior. In a pair of studies, researchers at the University of British Columbia had participants play a "dictator game":

> The game is simple: you're offered 10 $1 coins and told to take as many as you want and leave the rest for the player in the other room (who is, unbeknown to you, a research confederate). The fair split, of course, is 50-50, but most anonymous "dictators" play selfishly, leaving little or nothing for the other player. In the control group…the vast majority of participants kept everything or nearly everything.…
>
> In the experimental condition, the researchers prompted thoughts of God using a well-established "priming" technique: participants, who again included both theists and atheists, first had to unscramble sentences containing words such as *God*, *divine* and *sacred*. That way, going into the dictator game, players had God on their minds without being consciously aware of

it. Sure enough, the "God prime" worked like a charm, leading to fairer splits. Without the God prime, only 12 percent of the participants split the money evenly, but when primed with the religious words, 52 percent did.

Language profoundly shapes the way people think. Benjamin Lee Whorf, a renowned linguist, used the Hopi Indian language as an example of this. Whorf believed the Hopi had "no grammatical forms, constructions, or expressions that refer directly to what we call 'time.'" Consequently Hopi speakers think about time in a way that is very different from the way most of the rest of us — with our obsession with past, present, and future — think about it. To the Hopi, said Whorf, all time is "now."

THOUGHT EXPERIMENT

Write a long story about something that has happened to you. Do not write "I" or "me," but instead write "this one" or "this body" to represent you, and "that body" or "that person" to represent other people in the story. For example: "This one remembers a Christmas with other bodies when this one was young that was the most disappointing Christmas of this one's life."

The words you use will let you feel you are writing a story about someone else, even though it's about you. You will feel strange and start thinking thoughts about yourself that you have never thought before.

I SEE YOU ARE PLAYING AT READING A BOOK

Joseph Campbell wrote that there is "a curious, extremely interesting term in Japanese that refers to a special manner of polite, aristocratic speech known as 'play language' (*asobase kotoba*), whereby, instead of saying to a person, for example, 'I see that you have come to Tokyo,' one would express the observation by saying, 'I see that you are playing at being in Tokyo' — the idea being that the person addressed is in such control of his life and his powers that for him everything is play, a game. He is able to enter into life as one would enter into a game, freely and with ease." What a glorious way to approach life. What has to be done is attacked with such a will that in the performance one is literally "in play." That is the attitude described by Nietzsche as love of one's fate.

Ralph Summy, who directs the Matsunaga Institute for Peace, is well aware of the influence of language and encourages students to replace violent emotions by replacing violent expressions with non-violent language. Instead of describing someone as "shooting a hole in an argument," he suggests, this person could be described as "unraveling a ball of yarn." Summy also recommends that the expression "to kill two birds with one stone" be replaced by "to stroke two birds with one hand." "Dressed to kill," he adds, might become "dressed to thrill." Summy's work with language suggests that, by paying attention and substituting nonviolent for violent words, we can change attitudes and have a kinder dialogue.

THOUGHT EXPERIMENT

Consider our relationship with animals. Most of us typically regard ourselves as superior to other animals, which we see as lower forms of life. We see them as "its." In contrast, the Algonquin and Lakota Sioux regard animals as equal to humans, and in many ways superior, as expressed in their language. They address all life — anything animate or dynamic — as "thou," as objects of reverence: the trees, the rivers, the buffalo.

You can address anything as "thou." The ego that perceives "thou" is not the same ego that perceives "it." Whenever you see an animal, silently think the words "thou dog," "thou bird," or whatever term fits. Try it for a day or so to see for yourself. You will feel a dramatic change in your perception of all life.

Language patterns affect our perception, attitude, behavior, and how we live our lives. These language patterns are commonly referred to as "modal operators" by practitioners of neurolinguistic programming (NLP). The concept of language patterns being used as modal operators was comprehensively explored by Lubomír Dolezel in *Heterocosmica* (1998), which is based on the idea of possible worlds.

These language patterns are mostly verbs and adverbs that imply possibility, impossibility, necessity, certainty, and desires. Patterns of necessity are words such as *must have, must, should, ought, got to*, and so on. Speaking with these patterns, we create a world of force, pressure, and obligation. Patterns of possibility are words such as *can, will, may, would, could, want to, love to*, and so on. Speaking with these patterns, we create a world that allows human will, intention, and choice. Patterns of impossibility are words such as *unable to, can't, couldn't, impossible to*, and so on. Speaking with these patterns, we create a world of negativity, helplessness, and hopelessness.

The following thought experiment uses language patterns to influence your psychology about the way you feel about becoming a creative thinker.

THOUGHT EXPERIMENT

There is a pattern of words that expresses the contingent relationships we believe to exist between ourselves, others, and outcomes. For example, to say, "I can't be creative," is to say that there are some (as yet unstated) contingencies that make it impossible for the speaker to "be creative." What is being expressed here is a word pattern of impossibility.

This perception is more than a mere statement of conditions, for along with it come certain subjective relationships that can greatly influence an individual's behavior. Patterns of impossibility, for instance, presuppose a cessation of action. You stop striving for it. The other language patterns are those of possibility, necessity, certainty, and desire. Following are some of the most common terms in each of the categories:

IMPOSSIBILITY	POSSIBILITY	NECESSITY	CERTAINTY	DESIRE
impossible	possible	necessary	will	wish
unable to	can	should	won't	would
can't	could	must	am	want
couldn't	might	have to	is	choose
	able to	need		
		ought to		

Each of these terms presupposes a certain kind of contingent relationship between oneself, others, and outcomes. The outcome is either impossible, possible, necessary, certain, or desired.

Each of the terms conveys certain qualities of subjective experience that make the term unique and indispensable in understanding the current psychodynamics out of which an individual is operating. These subtle, yet utterly compelling, differences are immediately evident when you apply different terms to the same content. For example:

- I can't be creative.
- I want to be creative.
- I can be creative.
- I'm able to be creative.
- I should be creative.
- I need to be creative.
- I will be creative.

If you take a few moments to say each of the above sentences as though each were true for you (attending to your subjective experience as you do so),

THOUGHT EXPERIMENT (*CONTINUED*)

you will discover that each of the verbs dramatically alters your perception of your relationship to the outcome of becoming creative. The experience of "I want to be creative" is quite different from the experience of "I will be creative." The first assumes desire, the second assumes certainty, and there is a significant difference between them in terms of the level of active involvement each assumes. For most people, "I want to be creative" is inherently a more passive experience than "I will be creative."

Test out this difference for yourself. Think of something you "need," then tell yourself it is something you "should" have. How does your subjective experience shift? Next, select something you "should" have, then tell yourself that it is something you "need." Again, how does your experience shift?

This exercise provides clues as to what a person needs in terms of a change. For example, if a person were to say, "Yes, I'm sure that, given what I know now, I could become more creative," she would not be saying that she will become more creative, only that it now seems possible.

POLITICALLY CORRECT SPEECH

You may have read George Orwell's classic book *1984*, which focuses on the way people can be misled and persuaded by language when a political force with an agenda subtly alters definitions, censors words, and creates new terms. In the story, each word was rigorously defined. For example, the word *free* was restricted to such uses as "a field free from weeds" and "a dog free from fleas." There were no longer any words with which to express such concepts as political or academic freedom or the ability to think in a free way. All this was intended to alienate people from independent thought and self-reliance and clear the way for the government to control them. That was fiction.

What is not fiction is the way the present-day language police have established an elaborate protocol for what historian Diane Ravitch calls "beneficent censorship." Politically correct "school boards, and bias and sensitivity committees, now review, abridge, and censor texts that, in their opinion, contain potentially offensive words, topics, and imagery."

Below is a funny cartoon that is culturally, ethnically, religiously, and politically correct and gender neutral. Please enjoy it responsibly.

In her book, *The Language Police*, Ravitch reveals how absurd the politically correct censors have become. Following is a typical list of publishers' instructions concerning what they cannot publish:

- Women cannot be depicted as caregivers or doing household chores.
- Men cannot be lawyers or doctors or plumbers. They must be nurturing helpmates.
- Old people cannot be feeble or dependent; they must jog or repair the roof.
- A story that is set in the mountains discriminates against students from flatlands.
- Children cannot be shown as disobedient or in conflict with adults.

- Cake cannot appear in a story, because it is not nutritious.
- The word "jungle" must not be used. Use "rainforest" instead.
- The expression "soul food" must never be used.
- There are no widows or housewives.

Notice how politically correct expressions are expressions of "what is not." It is not a hut. It is a small house. He is not an old man. There are no mountains. Cake does not exist. There are no jungles. And so on. These expressions distort language in an effort to avoid giving offense. Even the word *brainstorming* has been condemned as offensive to people who suffer seizures. As a result of this politically correct language, our free speech has become restricted, and as a result, our worldview is becoming fragmented, petty, and false.

13 YOU BECOME WHAT YOU PRETEND TO BE

We don't stop playing because we grow old;
we grow old because we stop playing.

— GEORGE BERNARD SHAW

As I've pointed out, our attitudes influence our behavior. But it's also true that our behavior can influence our attitudes. Tibetan monks say their prayers by whirling their prayer wheels, on which their prayers are inscribed. The whirling wheels spin the prayers into divine space. Sometimes, a monk will keep a dozen or so prayer wheels rotating, like a juggling act in which whirling plates are balanced on top of tall, thin sticks.

Many novice monks are not all that emotionally or spiritually involved at first. The novice may be thinking about his family, his doubts about his religious vocation, or something else while going through the motions of spinning his prayer wheel. But when the novice adopts the pose of a monk, when he makes his intentions obvious to himself and others by playing a role, his brain will soon follow. It is not enough for the novice to have the intention of becoming a monk: he must act like a monk and rotate the prayer wheels.

The Greek philosopher Diogenes was once noticed begging a statue. His friends were puzzled and alarmed at this behavior. Asked the reason for this pointless behavior, Diogenes replied, "I am practicing the art of being rejected." By pretending to be rejected continually by the statue, Diogenes was learning to understand the mind of a beggar. Every time we pretend to have an attitude and go through the motions, we trigger the emotions we pretend to have and strengthen the attitude we wish to cultivate.

You can change the way you see yourself, and the way others see you, by your intention and by going through the motions. To discover how easily you can do this, practice the following experiment.

THOUGHT EXPERIMENT

"Practice random acts of kindness" is a phrase that someone in San Francisco wrote on an index card and taped to a friend's refrigerator. The next morning when she stopped at the Bay Bridge tollbooth, she smiled and said, "I'm paying for myself, and for the six cars behind me." One after another, the next six drivers arrived at the tollbooth, money in hand, only to be told, "Some lady up ahead already paid your fare. Have a nice day."

The woman started writing the phrase at the bottom of all her letters, like a message from above. A teacher received one of the letters and printed the message on the blackboard. One of her students was the daughter of a newspaper columnist who repeated the phrase and wrote about how kindness can build on itself as much as violence can. He started reporting "random acts of kindness" in his column. His readers were thrilled to read stories with happy endings, including one about a man who plunked coins into a stranger's parking meter just in time; of a dozen people who descended on a rundown house and cleaned it top to bottom while the frail elderly owners looked on, smiling; of a boy who shoveled driveways for the elderly; and of a man whose car had just been rear-ended by a young girl, and who waved her away, saying, "It's a scratch. Don't worry."

You can't smile without cheering yourself up a little. Likewise, you can't commit a random act of kindness without feeling as if your own troubles have been lightened, if only because the world has become a slightly better place. Just this morning at the dentist's office, I told the receptionist that she had one of the most beautiful smiles I had ever seen. The whole office suddenly seemed brighter and happier.

Make today a good day by doing a random act of kindness. Can you imagine a society where people really care for others by doing random acts of kindness? Let's make it ours.

You become what you pretend to be. The surrealist artist Salvador Dalí was pathologically shy as a child. He hid in closets and avoided all human contact, until his uncle counseled him on how to overcome this shyness. He advised Dalí to be an actor and to pretend he played the part of an extrovert. At first Dalí was full of doubts. But when he adopted the pose of an extrovert, his brain soon adapted itself to the role he was playing. Dalí's pretense changed his psychology.

Another remarkable example is Viktor Frankl, who wrote about his experiences in a concentration camp in his book *From Death-Camp to Existentialism*. While most of the other inmates lost hope and died, Frankl reframed his experience by pretending to be an academic lecturer. He occupied his mind by creating lectures he would give after he was released from the camp — lectures that would draw on his experiences in the camp. He took a hopeless situation and transformed it into a rich source of experiences that he could use to help others overcome potentially deadening and hopeless situations.

THOUGHT EXPERIMENT

In an experiment, some people were asked to write essays describing themselves as positive, self-confident, and highly creative, while others in the experiment were asked to write essays portraying themselves as negative, timorous, and uncreative. Members of the first group were then asked to present themselves to an interviewer as positive, confident, and highly creative. Members of the second group were asked to present themselves as negative, timorous, and uncreative.

The next day the people were privately interviewed again, and this time were asked to give an honest, objective description of their personalities. Those who had presented themselves as creative expressed a much higher degree of confidence and creativity. The others presented themselves as unsure and not creative.

You become what you pretend to be. Saying and acting becomes believing. This means it is possible to change your attitude and behavior by changing the way you present yourself to the world.

Imagine you have jumped five years into the future. The *New York Times Magazine* features a cover story about you, the outstanding creative thinker of the year. What did you do to deserve this honor? What new invention, business or business process, art piece, novel, method, insight, concept, improvement, or solution to a social problem did you create?

The president of the United States reads the article and calls you on the telephone. He is going to make a speech honoring your creative achievement and asks you for advice on what to say. In particular, he wants to know how you developed into a remarkable, positive, confident, highly creative thinker. What else would you like to hear the president say about you and your accomplishment?

When you look at the lives of creative geniuses throughout the history of the world, you find that their behavior and their creativity are inextricably connected. An example is Michelangelo, who was hired to paint the ceiling of the Sistine Chapel at the Vatican. His rivals persuaded Pope Julius II to hire him because they knew Michelangelo had rarely used color in his early years and had never painted a fresco, which entailed a complicated process. First the artist mixed sand and lime and spread the mix over the wall. Next the artist applied colors but had to do it fast, while the wall was still wet or fresh. When the wall dried, the colors fused chemically with the lime and were called fresco. His competitors were convinced he would turn down the commission due to his inexperience with fresco. If he did accept it, they were convinced, the result would be amateurish, and they planned to use it to point out his inadequacies to the pope and the art world.

Michelangelo believed he was the greatest artist in the world and could create masterpieces using any medium. He acted on that belief by accepting the commission. He executed the frescos in great discomfort, having to work looking upward, which impaired his sight so badly that for months he could not read save with his head in that same posture. By acting on his belief and going through the motions, he created the masterpiece that established him as the artist of the age.

BEHAVIOR CHANGES ATTITUDE

Your behavior affects your attitude. Psychologist Leon Festinger is best known for his theory of cognitive dissonance, which suggests that inconsistency among beliefs and behavior causes uncomfortable psychological tension. One of his early experiments, which he conducted with James Carlsmith, dealt with forced compliance. The following description of the experiment is from *Non-Western Perspectives on Human Communication: Implications for Theory and Practice* by Min-Sun Kim.

Festinger and Carlsmith (1959) had subjects perform a task that involved placing a large number of spools on pegs on a board, turning each spool a quarter turn, taking the spools off the pegs, and then putting them back on. As you can imagine, subjects' attitudes toward this task were highly negative. The subjects were then induced to tell a female "subject," who was actually an accomplice of the experimenter, that this boring task she would be performing was really interesting and enjoyable. Some of the subjects were offered $20 to tell this falsehood; others were offered only $1. Almost all of the subjects agreed to walk into the waiting room and persuade the subject accomplice that the boring experiment would be fun. Obviously, there is a discrepancy here between attitudes and behavior. Although the task was boring, subjects tried to convince another person it was fun. Why? To the subjects who received $20, the reason was clear — they wanted the money. The larger payment provided an important external justification consistent with the counter-attitudinal behavior. There was no dissonance, and the subjects experienced no need to change their attitudes. But for the subjects who received only $1, there was much less external justification and more dissonance. How could subjects reduce the dissonance? They could do so by changing their attitude toward the task. This is exactly what happened. When the subjects were asked to evaluate the experiment, the subjects who were paid only $1 rated the tedious task as more fun and enjoyable than did both the subjects who were paid $20 to lie and the subjects in a control group who were not required to lie about the task. Because the external justification — the $1 payment — was too low to justify the counter-attitudinal behavior, the subjects simply changed their attitudes to make them consistent with their behavior.

Think for a moment about social occasions — visits, dates, dinners out with friends, birthday parties, weddings, and other gatherings.

Even when we're unhappy or depressed, these occasions force us to act as if we are happy. Observing others' faces, postures, and voices, we unconsciously mimic their reactions. We synchronize our movements, postures, and tones of voice with theirs. Then, by mimicking happy people, we become happy.

CIA researchers have long been interested in developing techniques to help them study the facial expressions of suspects. Two such researchers began simulating facial expressions of anger and distress all day, each day for weeks. One of them admitted feeling terrible after a session of making those faces. Then the other realized that he too felt poorly, so they began to keep track. They began monitoring their bodies while simulating facial expressions. Their findings were remarkable. They discovered that a facial expression alone is sufficient to create marked changes in the nervous system.

In one exercise they raised their inner eyebrows, raised their cheeks, and lowered the corner of their lips and held this facial expression for a few minutes. They were stunned to discover that this simple facial expression generated feelings of sadness and anguish within them. The researchers then decided to monitor the heart rates and body temperatures of two groups of people. One group was asked to remember and relive their most sorrowful experiences. The other group in another room was simply asked to produce a series of facial expressions expressing sadness. Remarkably, the second group, the people who were pretending, showed the same physiological responses as the first. Try the following thought experiment.

THOUGHT EXPERIMENT

Lower your eyebrows.

Raise your upper eyelids.

Narrow your eyelids.

Press your lips together.

THOUGHT EXPERIMENT (*CONTINUED*)

Hold this expression and you will generate anger. Your heartbeat will go up ten or twelve beats per minute. Your hands will get hot, and you will feel very unpleasant.

The next time you're feeling depressed and want to feel happy and positive, try this: Put a pen between your teeth, in far enough so that it stretches the edges of your mouth out to the left and right without feeling uncomfortable. Hold it there for five minutes or so. You'll find yourself inexplicably in a happy mood. Then try walking with long strides and looking straight ahead. You will amaze yourself at how fast your facial expressions can change your emotions.

In a further experiment, the CIA researchers had one group of subjects listen to recordings of top comedians and look at a series of cartoons. At the same time, each person held a pen pressed between his or her lips — an action that makes it impossible to smile. Individuals in another group each held a pen between his or her teeth, which had the opposite effect and made them smile.

The people with the pens between their teeth rated the comedians and cartoons as much funnier than the other group did. What's more, the people in neither group knew they were making expressions of emotion. Amazingly, an expression you do not even know you have can create an emotion that you did not deliberately choose to feel. Emotion doesn't just go from the inside out. It goes from the outside in.

HOW TO CREATE YOUR OWN MOOD

Psychologist Theodore Velten created a mood induction procedure in 1969 that psychologists have used for over forty years to induce a positive mind-set, especially in psychology experiments.

It's a simple approach that involves reading, reflecting on, and trying to feel the effects of some fifty-eight positive affirmations as they wash over you. The statements start out being fairly neutral and then become progressively more positive. They are specifically designed to produce a euphoric state of mind.

THOUGHT EXPERIMENT

Velten's Instructions: Read each of the following statements to yourself. As you look at each one, focus your observation only on that one. You should not spend too much time on any one statement. To experience the mood suggested in the statement, you must be willing to accept and respond to the idea. Allow the emotion in the statement to act upon you. Then try to produce the feeling suggested by each statement. Visualize a scene in which you experienced such a feeling. Imagine reliving the scene. The entire exercise should take about ten minutes.

VELTEN MOOD INDUCTION STATEMENTS

1. Today is neither better nor worse than any other day.
2. I do feel pretty good today, though.
3. I feel lighthearted.
4. This might turn out to have been one of my good days.
5. If your attitude is good, then things are good, and my attitude is good.
6. I feel cheerful and lively.
7. I've certainly got energy and self-confidence to share.
8. On the whole, I have very little difficulty in thinking clearly.
9. My friends and family are pretty proud of me most of the time.
10. I'm in a good position to make a success of things.
11. For the rest of the day, I bet things will go really well.
12. I'm pleased that most people are so friendly to me.
13. My judgments about most things are sound.
14. The more I get into things, the easier they become for me.

THOUGHT EXPERIMENT (*CONTINUED*)

15. I'm full of energy and ambition — I feel like I could go a long time without sleep.
16. This is one of those days when I can get things done with practically no effort at all.
17. My judgment is keen and precise today. Just let someone try to put something over on me.
18. When I want to, I can make friends extremely easily.
19. If I set my mind to it, I can make things turn out fine.
20. I feel enthusiastic and confident now.
21. There should be opportunity for a lot of good times coming along.
22. My favorite songs keep going through my mind.
23. Some of my friends are so lively and optimistic.
24. I feel talkative — I feel like talking to almost anybody.
25. I'm full of energy, and am really getting to like the things I'm doing.
26. I feel like bursting with laughter — I wish somebody would tell a joke and give me an excuse.
27. I feel an exhilarating animation in all I do.
28. My memory is in rare form today.
29. I'm able to do things accurately and efficiently.
30. I know good and well that I can achieve the goals I set.
31. Now that it occurs to me, most of the things that have depressed me wouldn't have if I'd just had the right attitude.
32. I have a sense of power and vigor.
33. I feel so vivacious and efficient today — sitting on top of the world.
34. It would really take something to stop me now.
35. In the long run, it's obvious that things have gotten better and better during my life.
36. I know in the future I won't overemphasize so-called "problems."
37. I'm optimistic that I can get along very well with most of the people I meet.

THOUGHT EXPERIMENT (*CONTINUED*)

38. I'm too absorbed in things to have time for worry.
39. I'm feeling amazingly good today.
40. I am particularly inventive and resourceful in this mood.
41. I feel superb! I think I can work to the best of my ability.
42. Things look good. Things look great!
43. I feel that many of my friendships will stick with me in the future.
44. I feel highly perceptive and refreshed.
45. I can find the good in almost everything.
46. In a buoyant mood like this one, I can work fast and do it right the first time.
47. I can concentrate hard on anything I do.
48. My thinking is clear and rapid.
49. Life is so much fun; it seems to offer so many sources of fulfillment.
50. Things will be better and better today.
51. I can make decisions rapidly and correctly, and I can defend them against criticisms easily.
52. I feel industrious as heck — I want something to do!
53. Life is firmly in my control.
54. I wish somebody would play some good, loud music!
55. This is great — I really do feel good. I am elated about things!
56. I'm really feeling sharp now.
57. This is just one of those days when I'm ready to go!
58. Wow, I feel great!

You'll find yourself feeling good about yourself and thinking harmonious thoughts.

When you are in a good mood, you find your body exhibiting it in your behavior. You'll smile, and you'll walk briskly. Leonardo da

Vinci once observed that it's no mystery why it is fun to be around happy people and depressing to be around depressed people. He also observed a melancholy atmosphere in many portraits. He attributed that to the solitariness of artists and their environment. According to Giorgio Vasari, Leonardo, while painting the *Mona Lisa*, employed singers, musicians, and jesters to chase away his melancholy as he painted. As a result, he painted a smile so pleasing that it seems divine and as alive as the original.

Leonardo was onto something. Nicholas Christakis and James Fowler, professors at Harvard Medical School, conducted a study in order to discover who is happy and why. As part of the study, they examined a trove of facts dating back to 1971. What they found is that people who surround themselves with happy, positive people are not only happy but their happiness is contagious as well. It is not just happy people connecting with happy people; there is a contagious process going on. Likewise, every unhappy friend you have increases your unhappiness by 10 percent. Christakis and Fowler concluded that having an extra five thousand dollars in annual income (in 1984 dollars) increased the probability of a person's happiness by about 2 percent. On the other hand, a happy friend is worth about twenty thousand dollars in annual income.

CREATE YOUR OWN EXPERIENCES

Cognitive scientists have discovered that the brain is a dynamic system — an organ that evolves its patterns of activity rather than computes them like a computer. It thrives on the creative energy of feedback from experiences either real or fictional. An important point to remember is that you can synthesize experience, literally create it in your imagination. The human brain cannot tell the difference between an "actual" experience and an experience imagined vividly and in detail.

Two examples are told by J. L. Read:

Air Force colonel George Hall was a prisoner of war locked in a dark box in a North Vietnamese prison for seven grueling years. Every day Hall imagined he was a golf professional and played a full game of golf in his imagination. One week after he was released from that prison camp, he entered the Greater New Orleans Open and shot a seventy-six.

Another incredible account is that of Vera Fryling, a Jewish teenager who lived undercover in Berlin during the Holocaust while on the run from the Gestapo. During this time she imagined that she was a doctor, a psychiatrist in a free land. After surviving her experiences with the Nazis and the Soviet army, and a bout with cancer, Fryling ended up on the faculty of the San Francisco Medical School.

Fryling did not pretend she was a doctor. She imagined she was a doctor and turned her imagination into reality by acting the part. Her imagination was key to overcoming the horrors of the Nazi years while in hiding. Whatever you believe, you become. Reality conforms to your belief.

But most of us, when we look at our lives, see only what we don't have and who we are not, and we dwell on those things. This too is an act of imagination. With negative thoughts about who we are and will be in the future, we create ourselves.

I observed my mother overcome all kinds of adversity during her life. I learned a lesson from her belief that you construct your own reality. No matter how bleak our prospects were, my mother never complained. For her, whining about what she didn't have or complaining about the unfairness of life was a waste of energy. My mother realized that you create your own happiness by doing the best you can with what you have.

THOUGHT EXPERIMENT

Think of something about your life you would like to change or enhance. Sit back, relax, close your eyes, and fantasize what you would really like to have occur in your life. Don't put any limitations on it, and don't shroud it with doubt. Remember, no one else will judge this fantasy or prevent it from happening. Only you have the power to prevent its realization. If your fantasy is to heal your body, then imagine yourself as you have felt in your healthiest hour. Become that again, and relive it as a real occurrence in the now. Believe that you can regain your health, and this method will facilitate the healing. More and more enlightened physicians, among them Deepak Chopra, are expressing this. You have the power to do anything you want if you first imagine it in your mind's eye.

IKIRU

The Japanese film masterpiece *Ikiru*, by Akira Kurosawa, tells the story of an old man, Kanji Watanabe, a civil servant who has labored in the bureaucracy for thirty years. He determines his self-worth by how others see him. He thinks of himself as an object and spends his life preventing things from happening. He is a widower who never remarried, because his relatives told him he was too old and unattractive to remarry. He is the father of an ungrateful son who despises him because he is not rich. He does not strive to better his career, because he has been told by his supervisor that he lacks the education and intelligence to be anything more than a clerk. He pictures himself as a worthless failure. He walks bent over with a shuffling gait and defeated eyes.

When he is told that he has terminal cancer, Kanji Watanabe looks back over the wasteland of his life and decides to do something of note. For the first time in his life, he becomes the subject of his life. He decides to build, against all obstacles, a park in a dirty slum in Tokyo. He now has no fear and feels no self-defeating limitations. He ignores his son when the younger man says Kanji Watanabe is the laughing-stock of the neighborhood, and he ignores his relatives and neighbors who beg him to stop being a fool. He ignores his supervisor, who is embarrassed by the old man and pretends not to know him.

Because the old man knew he was going to die soon, he no longer cared what other people thought. For the first time in his life he was free and alive. He worked and worked, seemingly without stopping. Unafraid of anyone or anything, and no longer feeling like he had anything to lose, he gained, in this short time, everything. When he finally died — in the snow, swinging on a child's swing in the park that he had made — he was singing.

Kanji Watanabe became the subject of his life. He became joyous instead of miserable; he became inspired instead of feeling indifferent, and he laughed at himself and the world instead of feeling humiliated and defeated. He seized the day.

CONCLUSION
DANCING IN THE RAIN

Life is not about waiting for the sun to shine.
Life is about learning how to dance in the rain.

The other day I built a fire in my fireplace. I placed the logs in such a position that they formed channels for the draft. When the draft blew, yellow flames licked and jumped up the logs. Each log glowed with full intensity. When the fire died, it burned to nothing. There was nothing left but a pile of dust.

There was a world of difference between this fire and other fires I have made that were just piles of burning logs, and which had to be poked continually to keep the fire going. You might say one fire was alive and the others were dead. Yet we both know that fire is not a living thing. If pressed to explain why one fire was alive and another dead, I can't say, but I can feel it.

In the same way, Mozart's music is alive. So is the poetry of E. E. Cummings, the *Mona Lisa*, Steven Jobs's Apple computer, and a candle flame. In the notebooks of Leonardo da Vinci and Thomas

Edison, the sketches and ideas seem to have a life of their own. We all know that some business products, such as a Montblanc pen, are more alive than other products. The Nobel Prize–winning physicist Richard Feynman even made quantum electrodynamics, a dry, lifeless science, come alive with his famous diagrams.

I am, of course, speaking metaphorically. The metaphor makes us believe we have found a way to grasp this sense of life. Some people, too, seem more alive and creative than others. In the world of humanity, a person who is talking, walking, and working can be alive and self-creating or lifeless and drab. This is something we all know, yet never talk about.

What makes some people seem especially alive and others seem lifeless and drab? Look to nature for answers. One example is the emperor moth, which, with its wide wingspan, is the most grandiose of all the moths. Its wide wings span out majestically when it flies. Before it can become a full-grown moth, it has to be a pupa in a cocoon.

If you find a cocoon of an emperor moth, take it home so that you can watch the moth come out of the cocoon. One day you'll notice a small opening, and then you'll see the moth struggle to force its body through that little hole. The struggle will take hours, and the moth will appear at times to be stuck. If you try to help the moth by enlarging the hole with a knife or scissors, the moth will emerge easily. But it will have a swollen body and small, shriveled wings. In fact, the little moth will spend the rest of its life crawling around with a swollen body and shriveled wings. It will never fly.

The restricting cocoon and the struggle required for the moth to get through the tiny opening is the way it forces fluid from its body and into its wings, so that it will be ready for flight once it frees itself from the cocoon. If the moth is deprived of its struggle, it is also deprived of its health. Sometimes struggles are exactly what we need in order to become truly alive. When I think of people who are alive and joyful, I think of Richard Cohen.

You may not know Richard Cohen. He is the author of *Blindsided: Lifting a Life Above Illness*. He lives a life defined by illness. He has multiple sclerosis, is legally blind, has almost no voice, and suffers chronic pain, which makes sleeping difficult and leaves him constantly exhausted. Two bouts of colon cancer in the past five years have left him with impaired intestines. And though he is currently cancer-free, he lives with constant discomfort.

Cohen worked as a producer for CBS until he was physically unable to continue. Because his chronic illness and physical disability precluded him from engaging in many activities, it initially left him feeling worthless. Friends and relatives encouraged him to seek professional help from a psychologist, but he refused. He felt psychologists always focus on what's wrong with you and explain why you feel worthless. Like the emperor moth, Richard decided to use his struggles to become truly alive.

Cohen recognized the inevitable consequences of his illness, but he also recognized that he and he alone controlled his destiny. Cohen says, "The one thing that's always in my control is what is going on in my head. The first thing I did was to think about who I am and how I could prevail. By choosing my feelings on a conscious level, I am able to control my mood swings and feel good about myself most of the time." He cultivates a positive attitude toward life by interpreting all of his experiences in a positive way.

He said his life is like standing on a rolling ship. You're going to slip. You're going to grab on to things. You're going to fall. And it's a constant challenge to get up and push and push yourself to keep going. But in the end, he says, the most exhilarating feeling in the world is getting up and moving forward with a smile.

Richard Cohen is the subject of his life and controls his own destiny. People who live as subjects are wonderfully alive and creative. Once, on a rainy Sunday afternoon in a crowded café in Old Montreal, I saw a woman rise from her table and, for no reason, start to sing. She had a certain smile, and she was perfectly at home with herself. She was wearing a wide, white hat, and her arms were flung out in an expansive gesture as she sang operatic arias. Oblivious to her environment, she sang like a bird sings after a storm has passed. It was a moment when time stood still. Even as you read this, you may be thinking of people you know who are alive, and people who are lifeless.

This woman was wonderfully alive and self-creating. When you meet people like Richard Cohen or the woman in Montreal, you may get a vague feeling that you "ought to be" something more. You already know this feeling. We get this feeling when we recognize the thing in others that we long to be. We long to become more alive and creative in our personal and business lives. This is the most primitive feeling a person can have.

It is not easy to put this feeling into words. The person who believes she is the subject of her life is frank, open-minded, and sincerely going ahead, facing situations freely and looking forward to each day with a smile. The person who believes she is an object in life is inhibited, pushed, or driven, acting by command or intimidation, and powerless, and she can't wait for each day to end.

Years ago, I went to St. Bonaventure University in New York State to visit Father Tom, one of the wisest men I know. At the time, I felt shackled by my responsibilities, my family obligations, and the expectations of others. I asked Father Tom for advice. Instead of answering me directly, he jumped to his feet and bolted to a nearby tree. He flung his arms around the tree, grasping it, as he screamed, "Save me from this tree! Save me from this tree!" I could not believe what I saw. I thought he had gone mad. The shouting soon brought a crowd of people. "Why are you doing that?" I asked. "I came to you for advice, but obviously you're crazy. You are holding the tree; the tree is not holding you. You can simply let go." Father Tom let go of the tree and said, "If you can understand that, you have your answer. Your chains of attachment are not holding you; you are holding them. You can simply let go."

THOUGHT EXPERIMENT

Take a moment and imagine you are a mountain climber, and read the following scenario.

THOUGHT EXPERIMENT (*CONTINUED*)

You are climbing one of the largest mountains in the world and are very close to reaching the peak, which is a goal you've had all your life. You've prepared yourself physically and mentally.

You are beginning the final stretch of your climb, when you decide to rest on a small ledge that juts out about three feet from the mountain. You see another climber approaching you from below. He lifts himself up and joins you on the ledge. He's wearing a rope tied around his waist and holds the loose end in his hands. He holds out the end of the rope and says, "Pardon me, would you be so kind as to hold the end for a moment?"

You take the rope. "Thank you," says the man, who then adds, "Use two hands now, and remember, hold tight." To your surprise the man jumps off the ledge and yells, "Don't let go! I'll fall a thousand feet if you do." You hold on with all your strength. The man is suspended over a chasm, and sure to die if he falls. You try to pull him up, but he is too heavy. You offer suggestions about how he could climb up the rope. The man shouts back, "Hold on. Don't let go. If you let go, I'll die." You tug and tug, but nothing works. The afternoon is beginning to fade and it's getting cold. You have to do something, or you won't reach the peak, which you can see through the mist.

You think of a way the man can wrap the rope around himself and eventually pull himself up hand over hand, and you shout instructions. The man replies, "No, please, please don't let go. I'll fall to my death if you do." You coax, wheedle, scream, and yell at the climber, all to no avail. You think once again about the fact that you are running out of time, and you shout instructions one more time. "Listen carefully. I mean what I'm about to say. I will not accept responsibility for your life, only for my own. If you don't help yourself while I'm helping you, I can do no more. I'm going to let go of the rope."

THOUGHT EXPERIMENT (*CONTINUED*)

The man responds, "No, hold on. If you let go, I'll die. Just hang on tight." You wait and tug, and the man does nothing but hold the rope. He makes no effort at all.

You let go of the rope and climb to the peak of the mountain.

Now, take a moment and think about the scenario. What is it in your life that you are holding on to that is represented by the climber? What is keeping you from getting on with your life? Think about that thing at the end of the rope, and think about what it would mean to let go of it. Is it worth staying stuck in order to keep that thing alive? What would actually happen if you let go of it?

Once you can imagine yourself letting go of the climber, you feel a tremendous emotion. The power of metaphors lies in the fact that they speak to the unconscious mind. Metaphors encourage unconscious processing of information. Visualizing this story over and over will make it easier for you to really "let go" of your fears and traumatic experiences.

TAKING CHANCES

You have to take chances in life and let go of things that are holding you back. You cannot connect the dots in your life while looking forward; you can only connect them while looking backward. You have to trust yourself and move forward with your hopes and desires. As a child I was taught to seek security in fixed positions and prearranged strategies. One day, while approaching a stream with some friends, I, as usual, planned out my moves by visualizing how I would use the rocks as stepping-stones, putting down each foot on each stone in order to cross the stream. As soon as I began to cross the stream, I realized that if I stopped for only a moment I would fall into the water.

The only way I could cross was to keep moving rather than make a series of transitions between fixed stopping points. At that moment, I realized that security did not lie in grasping fixed positions but in continuous movement and flow.

Many of us who work in a corporate environment feel confined by its bureaucratic nature. If we were to let go of our fear of being fired, ridiculed, or demoted, and follow our instincts, what would happen? One person who did let go of his fears was 3M's legendary Richard Drew. Stories about him and his incredible creativity and drive are often told at 3M gatherings to inspire new employees. Lewis Lehr, former 3M chairman and CEO, said that if Dick Drew had not worked at 3M, 3M might not exist today, or at best it would be a lot smaller than it is.

Drew was a consummate risk-taker, constantly pushing to and beyond the limits of his job description. He ignored his boss when he was summarily ordered to quit working on developing masking tape and get back to work on improving a type of wet-or-dry sandpaper. That Drew ignored management and wasn't fired speaks volumes about both Drew and 3M's management philosophy even back then. It tells you that Drew believed in himself despite any obstacle, and it tells you that 3M's management had an intuitive understanding of the need to let creative talent alone and to gamble on their ideas.

After creating the initial version of masking tape, Drew asked an executive for permission to buy a thirty-seven-thousand-dollar paper-making machine. He said it would improve the masking tape, which was made with a crepelike paper. The executive, Edgar Ober, told Drew to hold off for a while because finances were tight and he didn't feel the machine was worth the expenditure. Six months later, Drew took Ober into the laboratory, and there was the papermaking machine, working away productively, turning out a vastly improved backing for the masking tape. Ober was flabbergasted and angry! He asked Drew where the hardware came from. Drew explained that he simply submitted a blizzard of hundred-dollar purchase orders over a six-month period. The machine was paid for with the small amounts of petty cash he was authorized to spend on his own. The machine helped make masking tape into a phenomenal commercial success for 3M.

Drew also encouraged his team of workers to attack their goals as relentlessly as he pursued his own. One day, one of his subordinates went to Drew with an idea he was excited about. He presented his idea enthusiastically and sat back to wait for Drew's response. Drew paused thoughtfully and then replied, "Your idea leaves me colder than a billy goat in hell." Before the other man's disappointment could set in, however, Drew told him, "You obviously believe in your idea so strongly that I'll fire you if you don't continue to work on it, regardless of what I or anyone else here thinks."

Steve Jobs, CEO of Apple Computer, is another example of letting go and living in continuous movement. His biological mother was a young, unwed college student who decided he would be put up for adoption at birth. She felt very strongly that he should be adopted by college graduates, and arranged for him to go to a lawyer and his wife. When Jobs was born, they decided at the last minute they really wanted a girl. So the people who would become his parents, and who were on a waiting list, got a call in the middle of the night telling them, "We have an unexpected baby boy; do you want him?" They said, "Of course." Jobs's biological mother later found out that his adoptive mother had never graduated from college and that his adoptive father had never graduated from high school. She refused to sign the final adoption papers. She only relented a few months later when his parents promised he would someday go to college.

And seventeen years later, Jobs did go to college. But he naively chose an expensive college, and all of his working-class parents' savings were spent on his college tuition. After six months, he couldn't see the value in it. He had no idea what he wanted to do with his life, and no idea how college was going to help him figure it out, so he decided to drop out and move on with his life. He later said it was pretty scary at the time, but looking back he recognized that it was one of the best decisions he ever made. The minute he dropped out, he stopped taking the required classes that didn't interest him, and began sitting in on the ones that did.

He slept on the floor in friends' rooms, he returned Coke bottles for the deposits in order to buy food, and he walked seven miles across town every Sunday night to get one good weekly meal at the Hare

Krishna temple. And much of what he stumbled into by following his curiosity and intuition turned out to be priceless later on.

Reed College at that time offered perhaps the best calligraphy instruction in the country. Because he had dropped out and didn't have to take the usual classes, Jobs decided to study calligraphy. He learned about serif and sans serif typefaces, about varying the amount of space between different letter combinations, and about what makes great typography great.

There was no hope that this would have any practical application in his life, but ten years later, when he designed the first Macintosh computer, it all came back to him and he designed the typography that was incorporated into the Mac. And since Windows just copied the typeface from the Mac, it's likely that no personal computer would have offered the number of fonts that the Mac had. If Jobs had never dropped out of college, he would never have dropped in on this calligraphy class, and personal computers might not have the wonderful typography that they do.

Steve Jobs was able to let go of the expectations of his parents and his biological mother, and to move forward, driven by his curiosity and restless desire to discover something more.

THOUGHT EXPERIMENT

Think of how you are living your life. Imagine that you will have to live it again and again, an infinite number of times, just the way you are living it now and have lived it in the past. Every pain, every joy, and every thought will be relived each time, in the same sequence, even the very moment of reading this paragraph.

As you imagine the eternal hourglass of existence being turned over and over and over, does this thought crush you? Or would reliving every moment over and over be the ultimate confirmation of your life?

Matthew Crawford thought about how he was living his life. He finished his doctorate in political philosophy at the University of Chicago and was hired by a prestigious think tank in Washington DC. After five months, he could not see the rationale for being paid at all for what he did. He was always tired, and he said he lost all self-respect while working in a job that had no discernible product or measurable result. Basically, he said, he was managing information, and his self-esteem depended on the opinions of others. Despite his income and title, he felt he was no more than a clerk.

Crawford quit his job and started doing motorcycle repair in a decaying factory in Richmond, Virginia. His journey from philosopher-intellectual to philosopher-mechanic forms the arc of his book *Shopcraft as Soulcraft*. Crawford states that an office is, at best, "a place of moral education," with managers acting as therapists, concentrating on making workers into "team" players. The individual begins to believe he is alone, and that he has no effect. He becomes passive and helpless and has difficulty imagining how he might earn a living otherwise.

The "massification of higher education" created this bleak scenario, Crawford says, where everyone must go to college or be viewed as stupid and/or unemployable. After you get a degree, you must take a job where you are "doing smart, clean, fun, and well-paid work." However, getting a job of doing smart and well-paid work is becoming increasingly difficult.

Crawford decided to do something that was meaningful for him, and became a motorcycle mechanic. He ignored other people's expectations about him and his PhD. To be happy, all he needed was to be willing to get his hands greasy.

Each of us is aware of the beauty of the potential that lies in us. We see it in the lives of Richard Cohen, Richard Drew, Steve Jobs, Matthew Crawford, and that wonderful opera singer in Montreal.

My favorite story about human potential is one I heard about a man who works at a supermarket, bagging and carrying out groceries. His name, I was told, is Johnny, and he has Down syndrome. One day the store owner asked the store employees to try to do something special for customers to create good memories about the market and bring them back. The managers and employees discussed their ideas, but when Johnny tried to get involved, he was ignored.

Johnny was used to being treated with indifference by the store's managers, so it didn't bother him. He thought and thought about what he could do as a grocery bagger. He thought about the things that made him feel good. His favorite thing to do each day after he got home was to look up a quote, or make one up if he couldn't find one he liked, and to repeat it silently to himself all the next day at work. Then he decided that, if it made him feel good, it would make customers feel good too.

He started giving his daily quote to his father, who would type it into his computer and print it out, giving Johnny multiple sheets. Each page would have many copies of the quote, and Johnny would cut out each one, sign his name on the back, and bring them all to work. While bagging groceries, he would put a quote in the bag and say, "Thank you for shopping with us."

A month later, the owner noticed that Johnny's checkout lane was five times longer than other lanes. He tried to encourage the shoppers to move to other lanes. Incredibly, the people wouldn't do it. They said they wanted Johnny's "thought for the day." Three months later, the owner discovered Johnny's spirit had pervaded the whole staff, and each employee was now trying to add an extra touch to make people feel special.

I often think of human potential, and how the courage and will necessary to overcome personal adversity can make ordinary tasks into extraordinary examples of inspiration. And when I do, I think of Johnny.

Use what talents you have.
The woods would be silent
if no bird sang
except those that sang best.

— ANONYMOUS

APPENDIX
RANDOM WORDS

Use this random word list with the technique described on pages 60–62 in chapter 6. The words are simple, visual, and connection-rich. Close your eyes and randomly select one (or more) of the words, then list its characteristics and all of its associations. (Refer to the guidelines in the chapter.)

bench	drum	violin
envelope	egg	candy
broom	meat	gutter
radio	cup	computer
landlord	umbrella	paint
cashier	hook	man
toast	door	glue
soup	window	water
hair dye	roof	bottle
beer	lake	neon light

shaft	football	knot	hook
prison	bridge	seed	magnet
bag	rope	weed	spaghetti
chain	pulley	bruise	disco
torpedo	toe	toilet	thumbtack
ladle	woman	closet	tie
insect	plow	shirt	sink
rose	mattress	pocket	bifocals
fly	sunset	pipe	television
fossil	gate	rubber	Jell-O
butter	clock	cancer	eye
nut	rash	plane	pot
twig	car	pill	wedding ring
bird	road	ticket	wine
sword	zoo	tool	taxes
motor	museum	hammer	pig
monster	painting	circle	hoe
dog	sand	needle	mouse
field	menu	rag	wok
gun	index	smoke	gondola
acid	book	referee	coconut
stamp	ashtray	sky	telephone
beetle	lighter	ocean	sleet
sun	hip	pepper	toll
summer	mouse	valve	notebook
ice	poster	triangle	dictionary
dust	aisle	thermostat	file
bible	milk	tube	lobby
shoe	horse	octopus	clouds
fog	tide	smoke	volcano

suitcase	cowboy	army	canyon
fish	tavern	beet	cards
lamp	butterfly	brick	button
library	cube	prostitute	riot jacket
university	X-ray	ketchup	film
fulcrum	money	explosives	runway
outdoor grill	magazine	diamond	flamingo
canister	screwdriver	camel	police
chimney	VCR	leaf	White House
rotating spit	stereo	train	lava
toxic waste	ink	lunchmeat	rain forest
coffee	ditches	liquor	island
ashes	razor	pilot	sunrise
groundhog	tea	lipstick	plastic
ribcage	eyedropper	caviar	Hindu
parking lot	actor	perfume	clay
lungs	homeless person	gum	gourmet
speech	queen	cheese	roast
math	artist	flame	heat
war	storm	fruit	limo
brunch	Indian	ham	campfire
sailing boats	snake	highway	fireworks
mirrors	fox	lingerie	tomato
burdock	lobster	jelly bean	tongue
sludge	Satan	bubble	fracture
wastebasket	balloon	choirboy	watermelon
watch	sauce	pet	Christmas
flag	acne	stethoscope	politician
helmet	crystal	eraser	quail
cactus	shrimp	bikini	handball

AK-47	ghetto	mushroom	doorbell
donut	bag lady	gasoline	marble
madman	ghost	music	knot
peanut	athlete	recess	pump
dance	herd	rain	umpire
song	flute	hockey	shark
congress	rod	eel	onion
arrow	constitution	rocket	garage
honey	handkerchief	barge	rum
bath	key	trash	attic
igloo	trophy	pyramid	fireplace
tub	zodiac	dome	deli
ruler	turkey	chapel	knapsack
nomad	surf	thunder	circus
subway	refrigerator	caterpillars	ant
Mass	dragon	jaguar	clamp
missing link	turtle	firefly	wrench
vein	seaweed	wasp	bum
truck	goulash	moon	software
monk	mud	moss	star
dinner	worm	panda	crown
label	planet	stomach	curb
laboratory	opera	brush	fingerprint
sandpaper	chameleon	gland	guerrilla
wedge	wart	intestine	iodine
sundial	olive	roach	jam
squirrel	map	exhibition	silver
mustache	coupon	holocaust	microscope
organ	foam	tax	nail
molar	nosebleed	lamb	piston

priest	podium	tile	ladder
doctor	scotch	piano	bus
salt	hat	skyline	toy
mouth	jet	creek	hair
horizon	soda	snow	rubber band
griddle	stoplight	biology	pond
candle	confession	cow	dream
banjo	roulette	bandage	pencil
anteater	spaceship	calendar	steak
tent	judge	calculator	template
funeral	soap	cake	compass
gear	dice	fence	tattoo
carpet	electrical outlet	toothbrush	insulation
windsurfer	nose	rainbow	legs
champagne	Apollo 13	apartment	wheat
salmon	bookmark	wagon	bread
underwear	torch	magnifying glass	paper
diaper	tomb	wire	soda
lug	can	dock	insurance
microphone	gold	rock	pennant
paperweight	ear	top	chess
griddle	beans	cursor	stew
rifle	spark plug	tire	waiter
paper clip	bat	drawer	goose
EKG	lawn mower	sock	sandwich
copier	pothole	taxi	sneakers
desk	bookends	zebra	chair
vibrator	fly	elevator	gutters
earrings	cuff links	stairs	zipper
shower	belt	branch	want ads

vest	ballet	laundry	drill
crab	shotgun	toolbox	orange
lottery	dirt	chopsticks	tobacco
rake	cream	bathrobe	myth
soldier	skin	conscience	journey
disk	spoon	chalk	child
necklace	swing	pool table	eagle
flashlight	skates	jar	costume
monument	curtain	bracelet	heaven
dam	wax	satellite	brain
teacher	hose	boot	minnow
bank	golf	helicopter	society
China	fortune cookie	fishing pole	examination
fan	change	rice	Genesis
steering wheel	atlas	puddle	skin
silk	phone book	wind	sin
earthquake	cuffs	comic	shadow
supermarket	vacuum	roller	cells
leash	courthouse	mat	hand
tea bag	chips	Volkswagen	sex
noodles	blindfold	safari	fire
theater	teeth	lightning	poem
mast	flowers	sculpture	blood
cabin	whale	board	castle
bone	chocolate	keyboard	psychology
buffalo	mantle	fig	Grail
kite	ball bearings	pole	symbol
hoop	lock	oceanfront	globe
archer	terrorist	town house	mow
hunter	dishwasher	angel	cross

intersection	hubcap	wallpaper	block
parent	carton	tower	screen
blueprint	sugar	kitchen	vase
forest	match	magnifier	basement
wigwam	deadbolt	garden	logo
iceberg	steam	general	torso
snail	saucer	eyebrow	pickle
jungle	Broadway	chapter	pigeon
log cabin	remote	catalog	whip
syrup	controller	bonnet	lint
	crucifix		
parachute	boxing glove	butcher	meatball
pudding	noose	dinette	tape
parsley	jeans	bed	coffin
ape	aerial	locker	meadow
sidewalk	crayons	professor	cyclone
vodka	pipe cleaner	cereal	lips
suicide	ribbon	cotton	watermelon
maid	pencil	brochure	knee
comb	sharpener	mime	swamp
picture	battery	elbow	furnace
	waist		
frame	wheel	medal	bingo
jeep	baton	fountain	weeds
Rolex	orchestra	fingernail	paper
mailbox	suspenders	beard	studio
shampoo	brassiere	student	patch
pendant	tractor	thumb	bleach
rail	candlestick	basket	cord
megaphone	newspaper	purse	pliers
skyscraper	secretary	arch	magician
skyline	salesman	cloak	faucet

mason	easel	thesaurus	office
jewels	flood	workshop	wand
lap	cockroach	cheesecake	graph
sweater	frying pan	gang	amplifier
band	crew cut	shelf	line
frost	hell	celebrity	bagel
girdle	miracle	leather	beef
stove	palm tree	snowflake	floor
hotel	choir	salad	barn
nipple	frankfurter	senator	dolphin
RV	trivia	bomb	aircraft carrier
grandfather	crust	airport	submarine
clock	oasis	cornmeal	reef
cruise liner	stream	cornstalks	casino
stage	hostage	manure	revolution
binoculars			
audience	dandruff	trumpet	bow
fur	rib	cone	kneecap
juice	popovers	temperature	borscht
buffet	dope	howitzer	raincoat
husband	frog	rally	dawn
bacteria	pilot	merchant	steam engine
spirit	milkshake	box	cliff
sauna	wheelbarrow	willow	seam
monopoly	level	stick	tumor
mold	aunt	canteen	zone
teenager	pimple	gourd	office
handcuffs	pizzeria	polyester	psychology
Tinkertoy	balcony	Stetson	Easter
chess	communist	minute	scar
scaffold	hedge	IRA	dancer

hero	breeze	mustard seed	nude
fear	postcard	symbol	trial
hamburger	beets	logo	traveler
welfare	photograph	United Nations	fraction
Vaseline	scalp	grammar	sausage
media	cremation	fertilizer	headhunter
laughter	network	feast	matchsticks
principal	scripture	cigar	fat
script	anchor	ornament	rabbit
contract	cauliflower	disease	duck
forecast	packrat	poppy	words
grid	cult	horseradish	cartridge
herring	dime	group	dwarf
warrior	robotics	strip	shuttle
occult	engineer	spinach	DC-10
putter	tar	dividend	bulletin
bush	maple	hospital	plum
tugboat	classroom	tank	check
bonds	pope	sonar	checkers
glove	statistician	sardine	FAA
wig	bomber	binding	wildfires
deodorizer	textbook	scab	bluebells
news	border	detective	vinyl
display	sagebrush	England	brakes
Internet	aluminum	dumpling	cavity
leopard	shutter	prune	pornography
team	safety pin	poker	landfill
staple	cargo	gravy	wages
hearing aid	lemon	mulch	vacation
expressway	garter	poetry	dial

CIA	eggshell	dynamite	parakeet
mosquito	Peace Corps	beam	pig hock
cherry	fugitive	supertanker	excrement
rattlesnake	gully	astrodome	vines
saxophone	Hawaii	cheetah	telescope
auditorium	lantern	Olympics	ostrich
timer	sulfur	trout	tent
dill	alligator	scissors	gold
cork	cobra	sand dune	jazz
condom	cattails	forehead	DNA
microwave	giraffe	Jerusalem	
rhinoceros	ranch	muffler	
marshmallow	vampire	resume	
scarecrow	emerald	chuckhole	
beam	confederacy	jellyfish	
scallop	cradle	liver	
pumpkin	alphabet	shield	
plumber	lettuce	fuel	
lizard lounge	reindeer	Japan	
official	paintbrush	lacrosse	

NOTES

INTRODUCTION

xv *Tired, he stepped into the shower in his hotel room.*
A detailed explanation of this NASA mission can be
found in Joseph N. Tatarewicz, "The Hubble Space
Telescope Servicing Mission," in *From Engineering
Science to Big Science*, ed. Pamela E. Mack, NASA
History Series (Washington, DC: NASA History
Office, 1998), chap. 16, http://history.nasa.gov/
SP-4219/Chapter16.html.

xvi *"I could see the Hubble's mirrors on the shower head."*
Quoted in Douglas Birch, "Hang On, Hubble; Help
Is on the Way," *Baltimore Sun Magazine* (March 14,
1993): 1718.

xvii *"It takes two…"* Quoted in T.O. Shaposhnikova,
Jacques Hadamard, A Universal Mathematician (Provi-
dence, RI: American Mathematical Society, 1999), 490.

1. ONCE WE WERE CREATIVE

6 *Martin Gardner.* Martin Gardner, *The Colossal Book
of Mathematics* (New York: Norton, 2001). For more
information about Martin Gardner, see http://
en.wikipedia.org/wiki/Martin_Gardner.

8   *Following is an interesting experiment.* The experiment, devised in 1966, is
    usually referred to as the "Wason selection task." See http://en.wikipedia
    .org/wiki/Wason_selection_task.

10 *the first image ever transmitted.* From Mary Bellis, "Philo Farnsworth,"
    n.d., About.com, http://inventors.about.com/library/inventors/
    blfarnsworth.htm.

2. THE SAME OLD IDEAS

11 *"Aoccdrnig to rscheearch at Cmabrigde Uinervtisy..."* For a discussion of
    this paragraph, the origin of which is unknown, see http://www.mrc-cbu
    .cam.ac.uk/people/matt.davis/Cmabrigde/ or www.ozzu.com/general
    -discussion/research-from-cambridge-university-reading-t1693.html.

3. HOW TO THINK LIKE A GENIUS

19 *pour water on a flat, polished surface.* The source of this example is
    M. Mitchell Waldrop, *Complexity: The Emerging Science at the Edge of
    Order and Chaos* (New York: Simon and Schuster, 1993).

21 *Who could have predicted . . . that ice would float.* This discussion comes
    from Thomas B. Ward, Ronald A. Fink, and Steven M. Smith, *Creativity
    and the Mind: Discovering the Genius Within* (New York: Perseus, 2002), 46.

24 *"God has revealed to me the secret..."* In Arthur Koestler, *The Act of Cre-
    ation* (1964; reprint, New York: Penguin Putnam, 1989), 123.

24 *"Combinatory play."* For a discussion of combinatory play, see Richard D.
    Smith, "The Effects of Combinatory Play on Problem Solving," 2005, Mis-
    souri Western State University, http://clearinghouse.missouriwestern.edu/
    manuscripts/544.php.

4. THE FIRST IDEA

26 *"a machine that counts"* Webb B. Garrison and Ray Abel, *Why Didn't I
    Think of That?* (New York: Random House, 1979), 20.

34 *Oedipus complex.* For more information about Sigmund Freud and the
    Oedipus complex, see http://en.wikipedia.org/wiki/Oedipus_complex.

36 *story of Helen Keller.* The primary source of this material is Helen Keller,
    Story of My Life, ed. Roger Shattuck and Dorothy Herrmann (New York:
    Norton, 2003).

38 *Think of the similarities between conceptual blending and music.* Walter J.
    Freeman, "The Physiology of Perception," *Scientific American* 264, no. 2
    (February 1991): 78–85, http://sulcus.berkeley.edu/FLM/MS/Physio.Percept
    .html.

39 *Jacques Hadamard, the brilliant French mathematician.* For an excellent
    biography of Jacques Hadamard, see J. J. O'Connor and E. F. Robertson,
    "Jacques Salomon Hadamard," 2003, School of Mathematics, University

of St. Andrews, Scotland, www.gap-System.org/~history/Biographies/
Hadamard.html.

5. WHY DIDN'T I THINK OF THAT?

42 *"The dogs were trained to approach something…"* For a discussion of the
experiment with dogs, see Robert Dilts, "Figure and Ground," 1997, NLP
Institute of California, www.nlpu.com/Articles/artic12.htm.

45 *The idea for "Dance Sparks."* The source of this story is Michele Root-
Bernstein and Robert Root-Bernstein, "Dance Your Experiment,"
Psychology Today, October 13, 2008, www.psychologytoday.com/blog/
imagine/200810/dance-your-experiment.

45 *Martin Skalski, a professor of engineering at Pratt Institute.* For more information about Martin Skalski and his work, see http://mysite.pratt
.edu/~mskalski/About%20Prof%20Skalaki.html.

46 *Tamas Vicsek, a physicist at Eotvos University in Budapest.* For more information about Tamas Vicsek and his work, see http://hal.elte.hu/~vicsek/.

48 *how birds of the same species flock and flow.* Bryn Nelson, "Swarm Intelligence Inspired by Animals," April 14, 2008, MSNBC.com, www.msnbc
.msn.com/id/23888902/.

52 *One solution created by David Graham.* For photos, a video clip, and a
description of the Move-it kit, see "Move-it When Shopping!" August 9, 2010,
Yanko Design, www.yankodesign.com/2010/08/09/move-it-when-shopping/.

53 *This perspective inspired a graduate student at MIT.* The source for this
story is MIT's *Technology Review.* See www.edkeyes.org/blog/050419.html/.

6. LEONARDO DA VINCI'S SECRET

56 *"In all cases of movement…"* Leonardo Da Vinci, *The Notebooks of
Leonardo Da Vinci* (New York: Oxford University Press, 1980), 37.

59 *"Fifty-five stocks are listed…"* This story was reported by William C. Taylor,
"Here's an Idea: Let Everyone Have Ideas," *New York Times*, March 26,
2003, www.nytimes.com/2006/03/26/business/yourmoney/26mgmt.html.
The article is a description of how Rite-Solutions built an "architecture of
participation" using the stock exchange model for employee suggestions.

60 *Mark Martinez of Southern California Edison.* Clive Thompson writes that
Mark Martinez found a new use for the Ambient Orb, and, within weeks,
orb users reduced their energy usage by 40 percent. "Clive Thompson
Thinks: Desktop Orb Could Reform Energy Hogs," *Wired*, July 27, 2007,
www.wired.com/techbiz/people/magazine/15-08/st_thompson.

62 *"Imagine if your daily consumption…"* Ibid.

67 *things appear to exist in a multitude of states.* This discussion of a multitude
of states of probability is drawn from John McCrone, *Going Inside: A Tour
Round a Single Moment of Consciousness* (New York: Fromm, 2001), www
.dichotomistic.com/mind_readings_quantum%20mind.html.

68 *The musical umbrella.* Article by Daniel Edmundson on PSFK, http://www
    .psfk.com/2010/04/rain-drum-umbrella-makes-music-out-of-rain-drops
    .html.

70 *Thomas Edison's lab was a big barn.* For a description of Thomas Edison's
    laboratories, see "The Invention Factory: Thomas Edison's Laboratories,"
    n.d., National Park Service, www.nps.gov/nr/twhp/curriculumkit/lessons/
    edison/4edison.htm.

7. CHANGE THE WAY YOU LOOK AT THINGS,
AND THE THINGS YOU LOOK AT CHANGE

82 *Most people think of perception.* https://www.cia.gov/library/center-for-the
    -study-of-intelligence/csi-publications/books-and-monographs/psychology
    -of-intelligence-analysis/art5.html.

83 *Not long ago, a man at a metro station.* This story about Joshua Bell's
    performance is derived from Gene Weingarten, "Pearls before Breakfast,"
    Washington Post, April 8, 2007, www.washingtonpost.com/wp-dyn/content
    /article/2007/04/04/AR2007040401721.html.

85 *Psychologists Ap Dijksterhuis and Ad van Knippenberg.* "Prof. dr. A. Dijkster-
    huis," n.d., Radboud University Nijmegen website, www.ru.nl/social
    psychology/faculty/prof_dr_ap/; "Applied Quirkology," *The Situationist,*
    May 12, 2007, http://thesituationist.wordpress.com/2007/05/12/.

85 *Focusing on the body rather than the mind.* From "Applied Quirkology," *The
    Situationist,* May 12, 2007, http://thesituationist.wordpress.com/2007/05/12/.

89 *A hospital is filled with hazards to your health.* http://www.nytimes.com/
    2009/12/24/books/24book.html?_r=1.

90 *Dr. Peter Pronovost, a critical care specialist.* The story about Dr. Peter
    Pronovost's experiment is derived from Robin Marantz Henig, "A Hospital
    How-To Guide That Mother Would Love," *New York Times,* December 23,
    2009, http://www.nytimes.com/2009/12/24/books/24book.html?_r=1. For
    more information about Dr. Pronovost see www.hopkinsmedicine.org/
    anesthesiology/Headlines/news_20080502_pronovost.cfm.

93 *Recently, the administration at Ripon College.* See "Ripon College Bike Pro-
    gram Entices New Students to 'Just Say No' — to Cars," February 12, 2008,
    Ripon College website, press release, www.ripon.edu/news/2007-08/
    velorution_021208.html.

94 *"varnish made of a polymer..."* http://www.newscientist.com/article/
    dn13592-intelligent-paint-turns-roads-pink-in-icy-conditions.html?
    feedId=online-news_rss20varnish%20made%20of%20a%20polymer%20
    containing%20a%20thermochromic.

8. TICKTOCK OR TOCKTICK

101 *Nicholas of Cusa made the following observation.* This discussion is derived
    from Robert A. Nowlan, "Nicholas of Cusa," n.d., from the series A Chronicle

of Mathematical People, www.robertnowlan.com/pdfs/Cusa,%20Nicholas
%20of.pdf.

103 *A speaker at an international seminar about world peace.* Speech by Dr. Saeb
Erekat on October 22, 2007, as reported at http://www.palestine-pmc.com/
details.asp?cat=6&id=233.

104 *The British artist Paul Curtis.* Richard Morgan, "Reverse Grafitti," *New York
Times Magazine,* December 10, 2006, http://www.nytimes.com/2006/12/10/
magazine/10section3a.t-7.html.

105 *Experimenting with cinnamon.* Kenneth Chang, "Cinnamon Is Key Ingredi-
ent in Anti-Mold Wrapper," *New York Times,* September 2, 2008, http://
www.nytimes.com/2008/09/02/science/02obsbread
.html?scp=1&sq=%22anti-mold%20wrapper%22&st=cse.

107 *Cemex, the big Mexican cement producer.* Keith Hammon, "A Lever Long
Enough to Move the World," *Fast Company,* January 1, 2005, http://www
.fastcompany.com/magazine/90/open_ashoka.html.

108 *slower is faster.* This discussion of crowd organization comes from Dirk
Helbing, Lubos Buzna, Anders Johansson, and Torsten Werner, "Self-
Organized Pedestrian Crowd Dynamics: Experiments, Simulations, and
Design Solutions," *Journal of Transportation Science* 39, no. 1 (February
2005), http://portal.acm.org/citation.cfm?id=1247227.

109 *Dr. Randas Batista in Curitiba, Brazil.* Dr. Batista's work was reported in
Derek Gordon, "Too Big a Heart," *Time,* October 1, 1997, www.time.com/
time/magazine/article/0,9171,987098,00.html.

110 *"A few years ago I was in Phoenixville, Pennsylvania..."* As reported by
George B. Dyson on The Edge Reality Club, http://www.edge.org/
discourse/self.html.

111 *Think about the business paradox.* Kenneth R. Thompson, "Confronting the
Paradoxes in a Total Quality Environment," *Organizational Dynamics* 26
(Winter 1998).

9. THINKING THE UNTHINKABLE

116 *the Roman war chariots.* There are many versions of this story about the
railroad gauge. Following are two credible references: "Roman Chariots,
Railroad Tracks, Milspecs, and Urban Legends," n.d., National Aeronautics
and Space Administration, https://standards.nasa.gov/documents/Roman
Chariots.pdf; and Cecil Adams, "Was Standard Railroad Gauge (4'8½")
Determined by Roman Chariot Ruts?" February 18, 2000, The Straight
Dope, www.straightdope.com/columns/read/2538/was-standard-railroad
-gauge-48-determined-by-roman-chariot-ruts.

118 *"Unilever corporation to place GPS devices..."* Naresh Kumar, "Unilever's
Brazilian Detergent to Stalk Its Customers," PSFK.com, August 4, 2010,
http://www.psfk.com/2010/08/unilevers-brazilian-detergent-to-stalk-its
-customers.html.

118 *Spencer Silver, a 3M chemist.* This comment and story are widely quoted,

though no source could be found where a print version of the quotation from Mr. Silver existed.

121   *developed by the director of the Tri-City Red Cross.* Jacques Von Lunen, "Cutouts Help Kids Connect to Parents Overseas," *Bellingham Herald,* March 13, 2001, www.bellinghamherald.com/2011/03/13/1914426/cutouts -help-kids-connect-to-parents.html.

123   *This led them to develop an egg stamped.* "Hi-tech ink perfects egg boiling," BBC News, July 31, 2006, http://news.bbc.co.uk/2/hi/5226338.stm.

124   *Using his imagination, Walt Disney.* Robert Dilts discusses Disney in "Walt Disney: Strategies of Genius," 1996, NLP Institute of California, www.nlpu .com/Articles/article7.htm.

126   *The following table illusion.* Roger N. Shepard, "Psychophysical Complementarity," in *Perceptual Organization,* ed. Michael Kubovy and James R. Pomerantz (Hillsdale, NJ: Lawrence Erlbaum Associates, 1981), 279–342.

130   *Japanese engineers for Toyota are working on a car.* Chris Ballard, "The Car That Emotes," *New York Times,* December 12, 2004, http://www.nytimes .com/2004/12/12/magazine/12CAR.html.

10. IDEAS FROM GOD

132   *after a period of incubating their ideas.* Leslie Berlin, "We'll Fill This Space, but First a Nap," *New York Times,* September 27, 2008, http://www.nytimes .com/2008/09/28/technology/28proto.html.

133   *The secretary who started the practice.* Clive Thompson, "The Eyes of Honesty," *New York Times,* December 10, 2006, http://www.nytimes .com/2006/12/10/magazine/10section1C.t-3.html.

134   *In the 1970s, Frank Wilczek.* Sharon Begley, "The Puzzle of Genius," *Newsweek,* June 28, 1993, http://www.newsweek.com/1993/06/27/the-puzzle-of -genius.html.

134   *Bertrand Russell wrote in* The Conquest of Happiness. Bertrand Russell, *The Conquest of Happiness* (New York: Liveright, 1996), 63.

135   *"We all know what it's like to see..."* Paul Hindemith, *A Composer's World* (Gloucester, MA: Peter Smith Pub., 1969), 70–72.

135   *The French genius Henri Poincaré.* For more information about Poincaré, see "Jules Henri Poincaré," 2003, School of Mathematics, University of St. Andrews, Scotland, www-groups.dcs.st-and.ac.uk/~history/Biographies/Poincare.html.

137   *"Annual plants, which die after fruiting..."* Rupert Sheldrake on Edge.org, http://www.edge.org/discourse/self.html.

139   *Here are some of the shows and their planned slogans.* David S. Joachim, "For CBS's Fall Lineup, Check Inside Your Refrigerator," *New York Times,* July 17, 2006, www.nytimes.com/2006/07/17/business/media/17adco.html.

142   *Imagine an egg sitting in its nest of straw.* Silvia Hartmann, "Metaphor Story about Change: The Egg," http://silviahartmann.com/metaphor-teaching -story-egg.php.

11. INTENTION IS THE SEED OF CREATIVE THINKING

149 *A magnetized object consists of a multitude.* Francis Heylighen, "The Science of Self-Organization and Adaptivity," http://vub.academia.edu/Francis Heylighen/Papers/249586/The_science_of_self-organization_and_adaptivity.

150 *"large white structures in the Iranian..."* This discussion is derived from Justin Berton, "Hashem Akbari's Cool Anti-global-warming Plan," February 20, 2009, SFGate.com, http://articles.sfgate.com/2009-02-20/entertainment/17190759_1_global-warming-Carbon-dioxide-climatic-change; and LBNL Heat Island Group, "White Roofs Cool the World, Directly Offset CO2 and Delay Global Warming," November 10, 2008, research highlights, p. 2, Lawrence Berkeley National Laboratory, see at www.scribd.com/doc/51049354/CEC-999-2008-031.

150 *"Your brain processes only a tiny portion..."* Scott Adams, *God's Debris: A Thought Experiment* (Kansas City, MO: Andrews-McMeel, 2001), 117.

156 *"except one particular shade of blue..."* David Hume, *Treatise on Human Nature* (New York: Oxford University Press, 1978), 162.

158 *The philosopher Søren Kierkegaard.* This version of the story came from anonymous English translation as quoted by Athol Gill, *The Fringes of Freedom* quoted in Robert Hirsh, "Existential Heroism," n.d., Willamette Stage Company, www.willamettestage.org/from_the_artistic_director/.

12. CHANGE THE WAY YOU SPEAK, AND YOU CHANGE THE WAY YOU THINK

166 *"The game is simple..."* Marina Krakovsky, "The God Effect," *New York Times Magazine,* December 9, 2007.

167 *Hopi had "no grammatical forms, constructions..."* Benjamin Lee Whorf, *Language, Thought, and Reality* (Cambridge, MA: MIT Press, 1956), 59.

167 *"a curious, extremely interesting term in Japanese..."* Joseph Campbell, *Myths to Live By* (New York: Penguin, 1993), 122.

168 *Instead of describing someone.* These examples are taken from Ralph Summy, "Nonviolent Speech," *Peace Review* 10, no. 4 (1998): 573–578, www.informaworld.com/smpp/ftinterface~content=a787821627~fulltext=7 13240930~frm=content.

169 *explored by Lubomír Dolezel.* See Lubomír Dolezel, *Heterocosmica: Fiction and Possible Worlds* (Baltimore, MD: Johns Hopkins University Press, 1998).

169 *There is a pattern of words that expresses.* This thought experiment from Jeffrey K. Zeig and Stephen R. Lankton, *Developing Ericksonian Therapy* (Bristol, PA: Brunner/Mazel, 1988), 169.

172 *elaborate protocol for what historian Diane Ravitch.* Diane Ravitch, *The Language Police: How Pressure Groups Restrict What Students Learn* (New York: Knopf, 2003), 3.

172 *publishers' instructions concerning what they cannot publish.* Ibid. These examples are summarized from throughout the book.

13. YOU BECOME WHAT YOU PRETEND TO BE

177   *Another remarkable example is Viktor Frankl.* The full story can be found in Viktor Frankl, *From Death-Camp to Existentialism* (Boston: Beacon Press, 1961).

179   *Michelangelo had rarely used color.* Giorgio Vasari (1511–1574) wrote *Vite de' più eccellenti architetti, pittori, et scultori Italiani* [The Lives of the Artists], which was first published in 1549–1550.

180   *"Festinger and Carlsmith (1959) had subjects perform…"* Min-Sun Kim, *Non-Western Perspectives on Human Communication: Implications for Theory and Practice* (Thousand Oaks, CA: Sage, 2002), 71–72 .

182   *Psychologist Theodore Velten created.* The list of mood-induction statements was introduced in E. Velten, "The Induction of Elation and Depression through the Reading of Structured Sets of Mood-Statements," PhD diss., University of Southern California, 1967.

183   *Velten Mood Induction Statements.* You can find other versions of the Velten procedure with different mood statements that others have developed over the years for different purposes. One example is www.amareway .org/holisticliving/08/velten-mood-induction-elation-positive-mood -statements/.

186   *Nicholas Christakis and James Fowler, professors at Harvard Medical School, conducted a study.* This discussion is derived from Harvard Medical School Office of Public Affairs, "Happiness Is a Collective — Not Just Individual — Phenomenon," press release, December 2008, http://web.med.harvard .edu/sites/RELEASES/html/christakis_happiness.html; and Nicholas A. Christakis and James H. Fowler, "Social Networks and Happiness," n.d., Edge: The Third Culture website, www.edge.org/3rd_culture/christakis _fowler08/christakis_fowler08_index.html.

187   *"Air Force colonel George Hall was a prisoner…"* J. L. Read, "The Power of Imagination," 1997, Enchanted Mind, www.enchantedmind.com/html/ creativity/techniques/power_of_imagination.html.

188   *Sit back, relax, close your eyes, and fantasize.* Ibid.

CONCLUSION: DANCING IN THE RAIN

192   *I think of Richard Cohen.* Richard Cohen, *Blindsided: Lifting a Life Above Illness* (New York: HarperCollins, 2004).

193   *"The one thing that's always in my control…"* Ibid.

198   *Steve Jobs, CEO of Apple Computer.* Paraphrased from Steve Jobs's commencement speech at Stanford University, June 14, 2005, http://news .stanford.edu/news/2005/june15/jobs-061505.html.

200   *"a place of moral education."* Matthew Crawford, *Shopcraft as Soulcraft* (New York: Penguin, 2009).

200   *"doing smart, clean, fun, and well-paid work."* Ibid.

INDEX

ABOUT THE AUTHOR

Michael Michalko is one of the most highly acclaimed creativity experts in the world. He has given speeches, workshops, and seminars on fostering creative thinking for clients ranging from Fortune 500 corporations — such as DuPont, Kellogg's, General Electric, Kodak, Microsoft, Exxon, General Motors, Ford, AT&T, Wal-Mart, Gillette, and Hallmark — to associations and government agencies.

As an officer in the U.S. Army, he organized a team of NATO intelligence specialists and international academics in Frankfurt, Germany, to research, collect, and categorize all known inventive-thinking methods. His team then applied these methods to various new and old NATO military, political, and economic problems and produced an assortment of breakthrough ideas and creative solutions.

Michael later applied these creative-thinking techniques to problems in the corporate world with outstanding success. The companies he worked with were thrilled with the breakthrough results they achieved, and Michael has since been in the business of developing and teaching creative-thinking workshops and seminars for corporate clients around the world. His website is www.creativethinking.net.